The Outlaw Years

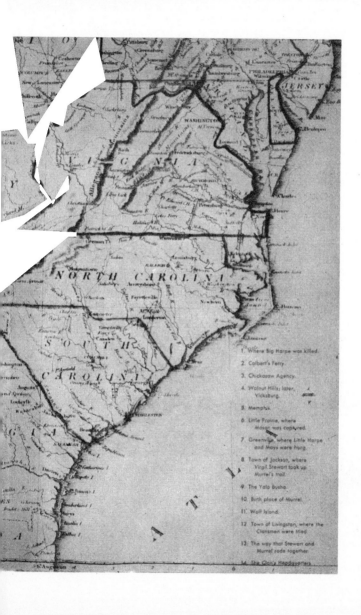

1. Where Big Harpe was killed.

2. Colbert's Ferry.

3. Chickasaw Agency.

4. Walnut Hills; later, Vicksburg.

5. Memphis.

6. Little Prairie, where Mason was captured.

7. Greenville, where Little Harpe and Mays were hung.

8. Town of Jackson, where Virgil Stewart took up Murrel's trail.

9. The Yalo busha.

10. Birth place of Murrel.

11. Wolf Island.

12. Town of Livingston, where the Clansmen were tried.

13. The way that Stewart and Murrel rode together.

14. The Clans Headquarters.

An early painting of the city of Natchez, by John Audubon, the ornithologist, who lived there for many years. The date would be about 1805.

The Outlaw Years

The History of the Land Pirates of the Natchez Trace

By Robert M. Coates

PELICAN PUBLISHING COMPANY
GRETNA 2010

*The word "Pelican" and the depiction of a pelican are
trademarks of Pelican Publishing Company, Inc., and are
registered in the U.S. Patent and Trademark Office.*

ISBN 978-1-56554-457-4

Printed in the United States of America
Published by Pelican Publishing Company, Inc.
1000 Burmaster Street, Gretna, Louisiana 70053

To
MALCOLM COWLEY
who had the idea

PELICAN POUCH SERIES

VOODOO IN NEW ORLEANS by Robert Tallant

THE VOODOO QUEEN by Robert Tallant

THE DEVIL'S BACKBONE by Jonathan Daniels

OLD CREOLE DAYS by George W. Cable

STRANGE TRUE STORIES OF LOUISIANA
by George W. Cable

CREOLES OF LOUISIANA by George W. Cable

THE GRANDISSIMES by George W. Cable

THE SHEPHERD OF THE HILLS by Harold Bell Wright

THE CALLING OF DAN MATTHEWS
by Harold Bell Wright

THAT PRINTER OF UDELL'S by Harold Bell Wright

THE WINNING OF BARBARA WORTH
by Harold Bell Wright

LEGENDS OF TEXAS VOLUMES I AND II
edited by J. Frank Dobie

PILGRIMAGE: A TALE OF OLD NATCHEZ
by Louise Wilbourn Collier

EVANGELINE by Henry Wadsworth Longfellow

EVANGELINE: A NOVEL by Finis Fox

THE NEUTRAL FRENCH: THE EXILES OF NOVA SCOTIA
by Mrs. Williams

BEYOND THE LAW by Emmett Dalton

THE OUTLAW YEARS by Robert M. Coates

A KNICKERBOCKER'S HISTORY OF NEW YORK
by Washington Irving

UP FROM SLAVERY by Booker T. Washington

CONTENTS

LIST OF ILLUSTRATIONS

The Outlaw Years

THE OUTLAW YEARS

PIONEERS

DANIEL BOON came first. He left his home in the Carolinas, in the Yadkin Valley; he came climbing up through the ragged Cumberlands, tracing his way westward "in quest of the country of Kentucke."

D.BOON
cilLED A BAR on
ThE TREE
in yEAR
1760

He blazed a history of his passage on the trunks of trees; he scratched his sign on boulders along the way: he moved out silently into the wilderness. He found it netted with buffalo paths, hunting trails —the Tennessee Path, the Bison Street, the Warrior's Path—which the roaming savages, from time immemorial, had been weaving through the forest. Boon went zigzagging through the maze. He blazed fording-places at the rivers, felled trees to make "raccoon bridges" across the creeks: thousands of other men, abandoning the comfortable prosperous East, came groping westward after him.

3

The Outlaw Years

James Calk keeps a diary:

> 1775 Mon 13th—I set out from prince william to travel to caintuck. . . . Thursday 16th We started early it rained Chief part of the day. . . . Wednesday 22nd—We start early and git to foart Chissel whear we git some good loaf bread and good whiskey. . . .

On again, from the little military outpost, along Boon's Trace. It is grinding going. One of the party wanders into the forest and is lost. They wait; they fire their guns and beat about in the thicket, yelling his name: he is gone, his fate unknown. The wilderness has gulped him in. Next day they move on again:

> April saturday 1st—This morning there is ice at our camp half inch thick we start early and travel this day along a very Bad hilley way . . . we cross Clinch river and travell till late in the night and camp on Cove creek having two men with us that wair pilates . . .
>
> tuesday 4th—Raney we start about 10 oclock and git down to Capt martins in the valey where we overtake Col. henderson and his Company Bound for Caintuck there they were Broiling and Eating beef without Bread. . . .
>
> tuesday 11th—this is a lowry morning and like for Rain but we all agree to start Early and we cross Cumberland River and travel Down it about 10 miles

4

"The men move out ahead, rifles crotched in their arms. Following comes the train of Conestoga wagons—the covered wagons: the 'frigates of the land'—with red bodies and blue wheels, trundling into the wilderness."

—A wood-cut from the Western Miscellany.

"A house-raising, a clearing, or a chopping frolic to establish a new settler brought in all the neighbors, who worked and danced. This was done gladly; in fact, not to be asked to one was an insult, to be settled at the next 'Muster' or County Court."

—*A wood-cut from the Western Miscellany.*

through some turrabel cain brakes . . . it is a very raney Eavening we take up camp near Richland Creek they kill a beef Mr Drake Bakes Bread without washing his hands we Keep Sentry this night for fear of the indians . . .

Food is gone: they have had hungry days, weary days; always, day and night, the great forest has been leaning all about them, breathing menace. But they move on, making their way westward.

wednesday 19th—smart frost this morning they kill 3 bofelos about 11 oclock we come to where the Indians fired on Boons company. . . .

thurday 20th—this morning is clear and cool. We start early to git Down to caintuck to Boons foart . . .

While some follow Boon's path, others strike off by themselves, trying to find a water route to the great Mississippi. Colonel John Donelson buys a flatboat and sets forth, his daughter Rachel with him—"a black-eyed, black-haired brunette, as gay, bold and handsome a lass as ever danced on the deck of a flatboat or took the helm while her father took a shot at the Indians."

They are fighting Indians all the way:

Wed. 8th. Cast off at 10 o'clock. . . . We had not gone far before we discovered a number of Indians, armed and painted. . . .

The Outlaw Years

A man named Stuart has chartered another flat-boat and is following behind them. The Indians fall upon him in pitiless massacre. Donelson's boat, drifting with the current, is powerless to return to their aid:

> . . . Stuart, his friends and family to the number of 28 persons . . . was at some distance in the rear. The Indians fell upon him, killed and took prisoner the whole crew: their cries were distinctly heard. . . .

Donelson's boat sweeps on, but the Indians follow, keeping pace along the bank, growing continually in force: occasionally, where the banks narrow, their bullets thwack against the boat's planking; occasionally, from some sheltered cove, a fleet of war canoes comes dashing to swarm about the clumsy barge. . . .

All these skirmishing attacks are repulsed: the men crouch at the boat's bulwarks, firing, passing down their muskets through the cabin ports for the women to reload. But still the main force of the Indian army marches along the shore abreast of them, waiting patiently for the moment when— snagged, beached or stranded—the boat will be helpless against attack:

> Monday. Got under way before sunrise. . . . We still perceived them, marching down the river in considerable bodies. . . .

6

Pioneers

Day by day, Donelson writes in his "JOURNAL OF A VOYAGE, intended by God's permission, in the good boat ADVENTURE"; almost every entry records an incident in this strange watery gauntlet he runs with death:

. . . Captain Hutchins negro man died, being much frosted in his feet and legs, of which he died. . . . The Indians keeping pace with us. . . .

Friday. We landed on the north shore at a level spot, when the Indians appeared immediately over us, and commenced firing down upon us. We immediately moved off. . . .

. . . The Indians lining the bluffs along continued their fire on our boats below, without doing any other injury than wounding four. . . .

In the end they outstrip the Indians but now another danger appears: jagged rocks fill the channel, and the current, where it is not boiling over hidden snags, has accelerated to that silent rush that rivers take as they approach a waterfall. They are nearing the Muscle Shoals:

. . . After running until 10 o'clock, came in sight of the Shoals. When we approached them they had a dreadful appearance. . . . The water being high made a terrible roaring. . . .

Every man takes an oar, the women helping: the clumsy flatboat swings into the current, yaws, and then suddenly is gripped by the water's force and flung rocking and careening down among the rapids. It goes scraping, straining, bumping—there are quick cries of command, frenzied heavings at the oars: over all there is the ominous dull thunder of the boiling river—and then at last with a sighing satisfaction they are safe again:

. . . Passed, by the hand of Providence. . . . We are much encouraged. . . .

They drift on down the Tennessee River, seeking the Ohio.

They reach the juncture of the two rivers, but in what lamentable state—their food, strength, courage all exhausted:

. . . Our situation here is truly disagreeable . . . our provisions exhausted, the crews almost worn down with hunger and fatigues, and know not what distance we have to go, or what time it will take us. . . .

But they go on:

Sunday, 26—Got under way early. . . .

Monday, 27—Set out again: killed a swan, which was very delicious. . . .

Wednesday, 29—Proceeded. Gathered some herbs on the bottoms which some of the company called Shawnee Sallad. . . .

Friday, 31—Proceeded on. We are now without bread, worn out . . . progress is slow. . . .

Pioneers

But they went on—Donelson to found, with James Robertson, the city of Nashville; his daughter, eventually, to take her place in history as the wife of Andrew Jackson.

And others came after them: Captain Hall, Major Winchester—famous Indian fighters both; the mighty Major Harvey: "his arm was as powerful as a trip-hammer—an Anak among men": he could take two medium-sized men and hold them up at arm's length; Colonel Bledsoe and Spencer, Boon's companion, who lived one winter in a hollow tree, shooting deer that came to a salt-lick at its base.

Few of them lived long, or died in any way but violently. Anthony Bledsoe was killed in July, 1787, his brother Isaac in 1793: both, fighting Indians. Two sons died in the same way. Captain Hall was attacked while moving his family to the settlement at Mansco's Lick; he and his son were killed and scalped. But while they died, others came to replace them. One sees them, their figures shadowy and gigantic, like the figures of men seen moving in a mist. . . .

"And as the emigrants came, the brawny-limbed, sturdy husband and head of the family was seen driving his pack-horse before him, his rifle upon his shoulder, his tomahawk and butcher-knife at his side, and followed by a stout, healthy, ruddy-cheeked, strong-armed, nimble-tongued wife, with a numerous train of greasy-faced, smutty-browed brats, shaking their tattered garments in the wind . . ."

They came by the thousands,[1] all sorts and conditions of men: mountaineers from the Blue Ridge and the Yadkin Valley—"the strength of their rough hands could break bones"; pack-peddlers, traders, army men, disgruntled soldiers—"the original settlers of Tennessee comprised a large number who had fought in the Revolution"; farm boys, city men, men of all trades—"carpenters, hostlers, mechanicks"; men embittered, seeking solitude—Aaron Burr, John Fitch with his despised steamboat model, Fannie Wright and Robert Owens seeking Utopia; proud fearless men and men with heavy secrets to

[1] At the close of the Revolution, it is estimated that there were not more than 10,000 settlers in the whole territory. The Federal census table, begun in 1790, reveals the astounding volume of immigration in subsequent years:

	1790	1800	1810	1820
Tennessee	35,791	105,602	261,727	422,813
Ohio	....	45,365	230,760	581,434
Kentucky	73,077	220,955	406,511	564,317
Mississippi	....	8,850	40,352	75,448
	108,868	380,772	939,350	1,644,012

There was something inexplicable about the whole movement—especially since, the East being at the time in very prosperous condition, no economic motive could be ascribed. European observers looked on in wonderment. A Dr. Raphael Dubois of the University of Lyons, constructed an ingenious device to prove that man, like the squirrel in a cage, is irresistibly impelled to step westward by the fact of the earth's rotation eastward. Others were content to mention, diffidently, "mystic forces" and "far-seeing powers."

conceal—"desperadoes flying from justice, suspected or convicted felons escaped from the grasp of the law . . . the horse thief, the counterfeiter and the robber. . . ." By water and by land they came, hammering their way into the wilderness, pushing on toward the scented River, the dreamed-of Mississippi, that lay like a liquid spine in the wilderness' midst.

Boon's Trace was the path that most of them followed: it led up through the Great Smoky Mountains and down along the Wautaga River on the other side to its juncture with the Clinch River; here the way forked. One branch led south to Knoxville, and so westward through Tennessee; the other fork turned sharply northward, climbed through the Cumberland Gap and, descending into Kentucky, curved gradually west and south again: this latter trail became known as the "Wilderness Road."

Both forks met at Nashville, already the metropolis of the middle valley, with a population of about 1000 inhabitants, all commodiously housed in cabins "built of cedar logs with stone or mud chimneys," with a post-office and a general store run by Lardner Clark, Esq., "Merchant and Ordinary Keeper." Nashville had "more wheeled vehicles than any other frontier town," and yet—so new it was—on any sunny day you might see its founder, old Timote DeMonbreun,[2] the French-Cànadian trader, strolling in the public square, wearing knee-breeches with silver buckles—"even to the end he favored the old-time clothes"—and showing off his plump, well-shaped leg.

They came pushing on, along one fork or the other, and the wilderness swallowed them; wherever they went, it touched them; wherever they settled, it surrounded them. Facing the wilderness—its dark loneliness, its strange menace; the bitter privations it imposed; and the sudden bountifulness it sometimes afforded—all men changed a little, as if their natures, like their mouths, were fed on the wild fruit it offered.

They built their cabins of felled logs: twenty by sixteen feet were the usual dimensions. Sometimes the floor was the bare earth; sometimes a floor of "puncheons"—logs split into planks—would be laid. Then, layer by layer, the log walls were rolled up

[2] This is not, even by comparison with page 9, a mistake; Donelson and Robertson did actually found the town of Nashville, but DeMonbreun had come down from Canada as early as 1760, and had established a trading-camp with the Indians on the site; he visited it annually until, finding Robertson settled there, he decided to remain. DeMonbreun was credited with being the first white man to enter Middle Tennessee, and the town was at first called French Lick in his honor, but even he could remember that there had been others. On his first voyage, he stumbled on a small party of wanderers. There were five men and a woman, and there had been a sixth—the woman's husband: he had fallen sick a while back and they had left him to die; a healthier member of the party had claimed the bride. DeMonbreun went on his way; the next day he found the man's body and buried him. The others had been heading vaguely westward: they were never heard of again. "This," the old trader used to say, "was no doubt the first white woman ever seen in Tennessee."

into place, notched and fitted at the corners. Two stout young trees, cut down entire, were set up at both end walls with their branches trimmed in a crotch to support the ridge-pole. The roof was of bark slabs laid like shingles, and held in place by a log for weight. Windows were rare: such as there were, they made of paper coated with hog's lard or bear's grease to let in the light; ordinarily, the clay chinking between the logs was knocked out in summer, for ventilation, and filled in again in winter, to keep out cold.

The interior comprised but one room, "answering the purpose of the kitchen, dining-room, nursery and dormitory." The furniture: "a plain home-made bed-stead or two, some split-bottomed chairs and stools, a large puncheon supported on four legs, used as occasion required, for a bench or a table."

The wardrobe was equally simple: leather hunting shirts, leggins and moccasins for the men, with homespun jean trousers, butternut dyed; "cotton stripes and linsey-woolsey for the women. If a calico dress was bought it created great excitement, and was 'norated' through the neighborhood." Children wore the "toga," a long shirt like a nightgown, the boys' having "two slits in the tail, to distinguish them from the girls'."

Victuals were measured by what the wilderness supplied. Salt was the great lack: "Salt was brought in on pack-horses from Augusta and Richmond and readily commanded ten dollars a barrel. The salt gourd, in every cabin, was considered as a treasure. . . . Often a family would not get more than a pound of salt a year." So meat was packed in wood ashes, then washed in boiling water, and smoked over the fire: "Cured in this way, it remained fresh as long as if it was salted."

Coffee was another luxury: "Ten pounds of coffee was a large annual supply for a family, which was used only on Sunday morning, none but the adults being allowed a cup." The rest of the time various roots, dried and browned in the oven, furnished a substitute. Sugar was made from the sugar-maple, but even this was rare: "It was only used for the sick, or in the preparation of a 'sweetened dram' at a wedding or the arrival of a new comer."

They rose at three or four o'clock in the morning; they went to bed at eight or nine o'clock at night. Rush-lights, tallow-dip tapers and the glow from the fireside furnished their illumination. Meals, though limited as to variety, were generous as to quantity. John Palmer boarded at a frontier tavern: for breakfast, the menu included "beefsteak, bacon, eggs, johnny-cakes, butter, tea and coffee"; for dinner: "2 or 3 dishes of fowls, roast meat, kidney beans, peas, new potatoes, preserves, cherry pie, etc."; for supper: "nearly the same as breakfast." After a cornhusking, a quilting bee or some other pioneer frolic, a collation such as the following might be set out: "hot cake and custard, hoe cake, johnny cake, dodger cake, pickled peaches, waffle cake, preserved cucumbers, ham, turkey, hung beef, apple sauce, pickled oysters. . . ."

But corn, above all, was the staple of diet with them as it had been with the Indians. At the marriage of Captain Leiper, one of the first settlers at Nashville, "the great delicacy for the ladies was roasting ears"; later, dozens of ways were devised to vary the flavor of the ever-present ingredient, corn meal: "Boiled in water, it forms the frontier dish called *mush,* which was eaten with milk, with honey, molasses, butter or gravy. Mixed with cold water, covered with hot ashes, the preparation is called the *ash-cake;* placed upon a piece of clapboard and set near the coals, it forms the *journey-cake;* [3] or managed in the same way upon a helveless hoe, the *hoe-cake;* put in an oven and covered with a heated lid, a *pone* or a *loaf;* if in smaller quantities—*dodgers.* Let pæans be sung all over the mighty West, to Indian corn—without it, the West would have been still a wilderness!" [4]

So they settled down: "clearing a patch and en-

[3] Hence, "johnny-cake."
[4] Curiously, its principal present-day use—in making corn whiskey—had not yet been discovered. The settlers drank Monongahela whiskey, flatboated down the Ohio from the distilleries around Pittsburgh.

closing it within a brush or a cane fence, upon which to raise corn for next summer's bread; when the day's toil was over . . . playing a Virginia jig upon a gourd fiddle, while a train of tatterly brats kicked up a tremendous dust as they danced over the dirt floor. . . ."

The wilderness surrounded them: black danger— of the Indian, the marauder—imprisoned them with the forest wall. Like a lens constricted to a narrow focus, their whole life lay within the circle of the cabin and the corn-patch: they hoed and reaped, rendered lard, ground meal on the hominy block, loved, slept, ate—"there, surrounding a skillet of grease, we sat with chunks of bread in our hands, sopping gravy, drinking milk out of a bowl with wooden ladles"—every labored gesture, like a loud noise in a narrow room, booming and reëchoing in their minds.

Gradually, as the settlers came pouring into the region, the danger of the Indians diminished; but now that very tide of immigration brought a new peril to the wilderness: the river pirates who preyed on the traffic of the River, and the land pirates, who infested the forest trails. As travel increased, their numbers mounted; as trade grew richer, they became more powerful. Everything combined to aid them. On the River, the current itself—with its snags, its shifting riffles and shoals—was a trap for the unwary boatmen; since one bank was under Spanish and the other under American jurisdiction, either shore offered the bandits a safe refuge from all pursuit on the other.

On land they were more fortunate still, for here the wilderness fed them, hid them, inspired them: its dense canebrakes aided them in the ambuscade, its thickets, its swamps and its reedy bottoms covered their escape and concealed their hiding places. They were the terror of the great trails—the Natchez Trace, where traders came back from the New Orleans market; the Wilderness Road, where immigrants came in from the East: Hare, and the two mad Harpes, Mason, and Murrel that erratic Napoleon of the outlaws—one by one they rose to power and had their period of dominion over the wilderness country.

They were its creatures, the bitter fruit of the same wild seed that bred the pioneers: they reflected, but in more savage fashion, the same ruthless audacity and fierce implacable energy which its loneliness inspired in their more honest fellows.

When their reign ended—when Murrel's fantastic dream of a robber empire in the West collapsed and the strength of the robber bands was finally broken —it was not because their own forces had lessened, but rather because the dark influence of the wilderness itself was at last being cleared away.

I

THE HARPES

"THESE TERRIBLE MEN, THE HARPES!"

ON AN April day in the year 1797 a young circuit rider of the Methodist Church was jogging westward along the Wilderness Road.

This was the track that Boon had followed. He had found it no more than a vague path, clotted with briar and matted with moss, but now more than forty thousand people had come after him: the Trace had been hammered hard and cleared almost to the width of a carriage road by their horses' hoofs.

On either side, however, the virgin forest remained unaltered: its great trees strode away illimitably, lifting their shaggy branches one hundred, two hundred feet into the sunshine; beneath them, crowded thick between their trunks, was the tangled screen of underbrush and briar, making a hedge that rose higher than a man's head on both sides of the way.

It was Spring. The air was heavy with the pale scent of flowers, and sleepy with the sound of the wild bees blundering among the lazily-unfolding petals. The young preacher—his name was William Lambuth—rode slowly: he was thinking perhaps of

21

the sermon he would deliver at the next settlement. His meditations were suddenly interrupted.

His horse shied, startled. Lambuth looked up. A man stood, rifle in hand, barring his path. "Stand where you be!" the man commanded.

The stranger was tall, broad-built, apparently toward the middle age; his skin was dark, almost swarthy—it had a peculiar "dried and lifeless" look; his eyes had the flat fixed stare of an animal. He was dressed like an Indian in fringed buckskin breeches and a ragged leather shirt. He did not move for a moment: unemotionally, he observed the preacher's agitation. Then another man, somewhat shorter and less ill-favored, stepped from the thicket.

Together, ominously, the two approached.

Lambuth began to protest: he had little money; he was a man of God; his cloth should save him from indignity.

"Git down from that hoss!" the big fellow ordered. Lambuth dismounted.

They took his horse; they took his pistol from the saddle holster. They turned his pockets inside out, taking what silver they contained. Last they took his Bible and fingered through the pages: occasionally, travelers would carry paper money pressed between the pages of a book.

Throughout the search, neither of the two men had spoken. Now, the big man flipped the book open at its title page: on it was written the owner's name, also the name of George Washington. At this the big man offered a strange comment:

"That," he said, "is a brave and good man, but a mighty rebel against the King!"

Lambuth, the first shock of terror past, had recovered a little of his assurance. He was convinced now that they did not mean to murder him; he began to reason with them, pleading that they would not leave him unarmed, unhorsed in mid-forest. They would not answer. They seemed as if animated by some hungry fury; they looked strangely at him. Lambuth began to fear again.

Now two women appeared, coming silently, both ragged and unkempt. This seemed a signal: the men bundled their booty together; Lambuth watching helplessly, they seized the horse by the bridle and made off into the forest.

As they went, as they entered the thicket, both turned abruptly.

"We are the Harpes!" they shouted, then plunged out of sight.

It had been a strange visitation. Not the fact of the robbery had been surprising: brigandage was already frequent along that barren way. But this one had lacked all purpose: preachers were always poor; the hold-up had not repaid its risk. Yet the robbers had seemed neither surprised nor angered. All their

actions had been erratic, as if half-controlled: they
had been like men throbbing with a strange fury.
They had been like madmen. Lambuth, pondering,
trudged on toward the settlement of Barboursville,
to tell of his adventure.

This was the first known crime of the Harpes. It
was, also, almost the only one that did not end in
murder.

Their coming had been dramatic in its suddenness. As if embodied in the wilderness, like an incar-
nation of its menace, they had suddenly stepped
forth, cried: "We are the Harpes!"

Later, research and their own confessions revealed
something of their history.

The two men were brothers: "Big Harpe"—Micajah; and Wiley—"Little Harpe." Both had been
born in North Carolina, one in the year 1768 and
the other two years later. There were rumors as
to their parentage; many thought them part Negro:
"their tawny appearance and dark curly hair betrayed a tinge of African blood."

In any case, it is known that their father had been
a Tory; he fought with the British during the early
years of the War. Later, as the Revolution prospered, he had tried to turn his coat, but his neighbors had too long memories: he was forced to flee
for his life. The two sons and the mother remained.

"These Terrible Men, The Harpes!"

Whether they suffered from the same spite is not known. At any rate, in 1795, the sons in their turn took flight from North Carolina, heading west. Two women came with them: two sisters, Susan and Betsey Roberts. Susan the elder—"rather tall, rawboned, dark hair and eyes, and rather ugly"— claimed to be Big Harpe's lawful wife. The younger sister Betsey was blonde, blue-eyed, gay-tempered, "a perfect contrast with her sister": she was wife to either of the Harpes, as the mood seized her, or them.

So, roaming westward with their little harem, the two Harpes made their way into central Tennessee. Here, through some accident, they established friendly relations with a tribe of Cherokee Indians— a tribe, wandering like themselves, outlawed for some breach of faith from the general confederacy of the Indian nations. They lived with the savages for two years: it was a dangerous life.

Hunted by both redskin and white, attacked constantly or attacking, they learned to strike with cunning and walk warily. Throughout the rest of their career, they preserved many of the habits they thus acquired: they dressed in leather, the women as well as the men; in a day when the tasseled coonskin cap was the badge of the white man, the Harpes went hatless—"except in the coldest weather, and then they used the kind they whanged together with deer-

25

The Outlaw Years

skin thongs." It was among the Indians as well, in all probability, that their blood-madness was born.

Many men, leaving the policed and prosperous East, had felt strange impulses strengthening within them, wild new instincts blossoming in their hearts. At home, in the cities, on farms along the Housatonic or the Yadkin Rivers, they had been indistinguishable from their fellows, but once they entered the wilderness they were transformed. Its perfumed appeal, its dark menace particularized them: as if in a kind of intimate abandonment—as if, alone against the dark heart of the continent, their own hearts unfolded—they revealed by their violences, or by their heroisms, how different they were from other men. So it was with the Harpes: if they had stayed at home, if their rage had never fed on the wild soil of the West, they might have lived sane and law-abiding. Seeded among the savages, their madness had its terrible flowering among the whites.

They had just deserted the Indians when they encountered the preacher Lambuth. After robbing him, they went on to Knoxville.

The young town of Knoxville lay at the confluence of the Holston and the French Broad Rivers, on the south branch of the Wilderness Road. It marked the overland gateway to the West: it was wild, tumultuous, booming. Half its population

26

"These Terrible Men, The Harpes!"

changed overnight as the emigrants entered, stopped
for supplies and plunged westward again; the other
half thrived on the trade thus fostered.

Rum shops lined the streets. "I stood aghast!"
wrote James Weir, who visited the town in 1798.
He saw men jostling, singing, swearing; women yelling from the doorways; half-naked niggers playing
on their "banjies" while the crowd whooped and
danced around them. Whiskey cost four shillings a
pint and peach brandy the same. "The town was confused with a promiscuous throng of every denomina-
tion"—blanket-clad Indians, leather-shirted woods-
men, gamblers hard-eyed and vigilant—"My soul
shrank back." The whole town was roaring. The
Harpes liked it.

For some time, however, they preserved the character of honest settlers. Arriving, they had taken a
small tract of land along the Beaver Creek, a few
miles west of town.

In those days, building a cabin, clearing a "patch"
were community affairs. All the neighbors came:
while the men worked—chopping logs for the cabin
walls, splitting "puncheon" planks for the floor, slab-
bing bark for the roof—the women would be quilting, twisting "hankins" of yarn, stuffing bedticks
with dried moss or pine needles, gossiping. In the
end, with the cabin raised and the corn patch cleared,
a whiskey jug would be uncorked and a gourd fiddle

27

would appear, and a rattling reel would follow, danced on the new-laid floor.

> *"Mush-a-ring-a-ring-a-rah!*
> *Whack fol'd the dady O!*
> *Whack fol'd the dady O!*
> *Thar's whiskey in the jug!"*

Such was the welcome the Harpes received and among those who came down to the frolic were John Rice, a minister living a few miles to the northward, and his daughter Sally.

Sally Rice had a frail blonde beauty; she was not yet twenty years old: Little Harpe was smitten with her at once. Through the summer, he haunted the Rices' cabin, paying his court in his hang-dog fashion; before the setting-in of Fall he had married her. Her father performed the ceremony.

Such men as the Harpes, however, with the wild energy that filled them, could not be satisfied with peace. They found outlet, at first, in petty thievery.

They had been raising hogs and selling pork to the butcher at Knoxville, John Miller. Now Miller noticed that they came in more frequently, and had more pork to sell at every trip. Soon they were always around the town, swapping horses and racing, drinking, gambling, carousing: imperceptibly, they had turned from honest farmers into rowdies, bruisers.

"These Terrible Men, The Harpes!"

People who had trusted them now eyed them cautiously and kept away from dealings with them: as if accidentally, a series of fires destroyed the barns and outhouses of these same wary gentlemen. Suspicion, gradually, settled on the Harpes.

Matters came to a climax with the theft of a team of fine horses from the stable of Edward Tiel. Tiel was a prominent man; his horses were prime: without delay he drummed his neighbors into a posse and set out to interview the Harpes.

The posse came too late. They found a deserted cabin, but the clearing showed the hoof-prints of a number of horses; a fresh track led away into the forest.

Tiel and his men set out on the trail, riding rapidly. Deep in the Cumberlands, they overtook the two Harpes alone, driving the stolen horses. The thieves made no resistance; they seemed dejected, as if befuddled. Triumphantly, Tiel led them back toward Knoxville.

Like all madmen, the Harpes were never consistent. In their flight, they had left a trail that a child could have followed. They had shown no spirit when captured. But now, suddenly, their cunning awakened. Unnoticed, they sidled toward the edge of the road, leaped free, plunged into the forest.

Their guards had only time for a startled yell of warning. Then—Tiel cursing, the whole troupe spurring about in the thicket, searching—the Harpes had gone. It was as if they had vanished.

A few miles outside town, on the banks of the Holston River, a man named Hughes maintained a tavern. Like most such places in that time it dealt in a variety of goods. There were bolted calicos on the shelves, a miscellany of hardware, a counter bake-shop. Meals were served, with grog or a bowl of toddy, at the fixed rate of four shillings sixpence; between-meals, drinks sold by the bottle and whiskey —"such as will sink tallow": thus was the proof determined—was the principal potion. There was no bar: instead, the proprietor stood behind a latticed wicket in a corner and the purchaser dealt with him, as now with a cashier at a bank, through an opening just wide enough to shove the bottle and receive change.

Hughes' place had an evil reputation: it was known as a "rowdy groggery," much frequented by bruisers from the river and skulkers from the town. On the night of Tiel's chase and the Harpes' escape, however, it was almost deserted. In those days men rose at dawn or earlier and went to bed at dusk: their lives followed the sun; as the lowering night came on there remained in Hughes' little inn-common only four men: Hughes himself, the two Metcalfe boys, his wife's brothers, and a man named Johnson.

Of the man Johnson, as of so many others among the Harpes' victims, nothing is known save the manner of his death. He had come West, and the Harpes killed him, and that single dark encounter is the only relic of his life.

He sat in the darkening room; he had drunk his bottle and was demanding more. Hughes was telling him to clear out, it was closing time. But he wanted more. And soon the two Harpes, come back to Knoxville on no one knows what crazy errand of their own, appeared in the doorway.

What followed—what thrashing struggle, what hopeless pleading—can only be surmised from the final outcome. Two days later, Johnson's body was found floating in a weedy ebb of the Holston River. The murderers had thought to dispose of the corpse in the manner later made famous by Murrel: they had ripped open the belly, removed the entrails and weighted the cavity with stones. In spite of their work, the body had floated.

Hughes and the Metcalfes were arrested; they blamed the Harpes, who had disappeared; they were acquitted for lack of evidence. At their release, the Metcalfe brothers wisely decamped. Hughes, with braggadocio, reopened his groggery: it was immediately visited by a party of "Regulators"; [1] the house was pulled down and Hughes, after an unmerciful cowhiding, was driven from the country.

The Harpes could not be found, nor their trail discovered—until it appeared in blood.

Some days later, just south of the settlement of Barboursville, on the north branch of the Wilderness Road, a man's body was found lying. He had been a poor old fellow, a pack-peddler; his name was Peyton. He had been tomahawked. His bundle had been torn open and scattered, but little save a few items of women's wearing apparel had been taken.

Farther out into the wilderness, and a few days later, two more bodies were found: two men from Maryland named Paca and Bates; they had been traveling toward Nashville. Bates had been shot in the back and killed instantly; Paca had been wounded, had struggled: his head had been split with the tomahawk. Both had been stripped of their clothing. The Harpes had continued westward.

About a month afterward, early in December, a young traveler from Virginia named Stephen Langford arrived toward nightfall at the tavern-ordinary kept by John Pharris on the Wilderness Road.

This was a meeting-place well known to travelers

[1] That is, a citizens' posse.

of the day. It lay just outside the settlement of Little Rock Castle: between it and the next town, Crab Orchard, the road traversed a thirty-mile-wide stretch of country which—torn by ravines, infested with Indians—was known even in that land of unbroken forest as "the Wilderness."

No man would willingly face it alone. Those who must traverse it waited until others joined them; often they advertised their intention by a scrawled notice tacked to Pharris' inn-door, or an item inserted in one of the early newspapers, as in the Kentucky Gazette: "A large company will start from the Crab Orchard on the 20th of February, in order to go through the Wilderness." Similarly, west-bound travelers met and joined forces at Pharris' inn.

When young Langford arrived, however, he found no others waiting to make the journey. To go on alone that day, the landlord assured him, was out of the question: he would be benighted in mid-wilderness. Besides, if he waited over, some other traveler might appear, to-morrow. Langford decided to stop that night at the inn.

Next day in the early misty morning, Langford, leaning in the inn-door while breakfast was preparing, saw a small party coming down the road. Two men and three women: they all had a ragged lowering look; they came lagging along, Indian-fashion, driving two spavined horses before them: across the

The Outlaw Years

backs of these were slung a few bags, some cooking-implements, a rifle or two. An unprepossessing out-fit, but there were two men among them; they were armed: better poor company than no company at all. Langford—he was a gay young fellow, high-spiritedly heading westward—hailed them jovially; asked them to wait while he breakfasted, and they would attack the Wilderness together.

The strangers picketed their horses, came tramp-ing silently into the inn. Soon Pharris appeared with a steaming platter of johnny-cakes made of Indian meal, a pot of coffee, rashers of bacon: "Ye can sit down to table," he announced.

The strangers did not stir: they had no money, they said. "You won't go hungry for lack of that!" declared Langford. "Sit down to your food. I'll foot the bill."

So they pulled up a bench to the table; they ate hearty. When the meal was over, Langford called for his reckoning; when he paid it, he pulled a well-filled wallet from his greatcoat pocket. The stran-gers watched him silently. Soon after, they all set out together, disappeared into the Wilderness.

Langford's body was found a week later: a party of drovers pursuing some scattered steers stumbled on it in the underbrush at the bottom of a ravine. He had been stripped, robbed, tomahawked.

"These Terrible Men, The Harpes!"

The Harpes now had five murders to their credit, spaced along the Wilderness Road like bloody blaze-markings of their passage. The cumulative effect aroused the settlers; a posse set forth from the town of Stanford, under the leadership of Captain Joseph Ballenger. They had not far to search.

Again—as, previously, at Knoxville—pursuit seemed to coincide with some curious subsidence in the Harpes of their wild energies. Ballenger and his men found them with their women—quite unwary, quite unapprehensive—sitting in a row on a log beside the Trace, a few miles out of town.

They offered no resistance; as if bewildered, they permitted themselves to be bound and led back to Stanford.[2]

At the arraignment, all the defendants gave the name of Roberts except Betsey, Big Harpe's alternate wife: she gave the name of Elizabeth Waker. The rest was mere formality; their guilt was plainly evident. Captain Ballenger, being sworn, affirmed that when he arrested them, he "found in their possession a pocketbook with the name of Stephen Langford, some shirts of fine linen, a greatcoat, various other of his possessions"; several innkeepers testified to their passage along the Wilderness. They were remanded to the jail, to await removal to Danville for trial at the District Court sessions.

[2] See page 307: Rothert, Otto A.

The Outlaw Years

Matters had now become a little complicated: all three women were pregnant, and approaching delivery. When they were carried to the Danville District Jail John Biegler, the warden there, was beset by the double duties of turnkey and nurse. Moreover, in spite of their aliases, the identity of the suspects had at last been learned, and their connection with the previous murders established; the little jailhouse was besieged by people from the outlying settlements, who had ridden in to have a look at "these terrible men, the Harpes."

Warmed by their notoriety, the Harpes swelled with confidence. Big Harpe boasted of his strength. He offered to take on any two men in a fair fight with fists, provided he be set free if he bested them. Everybody seemed to think it was a fair sporting offer. Biegler the jailer began a series of requisitions for handcuffs and iron-ware—balanced by condiments and infusions for the expectant mothers.

The jail—built, as ordered by the Court in 1784, "of hewed or sawed logs at least nine inches thick"— might have seemed sturdy enough to hold any ordinary criminals. A week after the arrival of the Harpes, however, Biegler's cashbook recorded the purchase of "two horse locks to chain the men's feet to the ground, 12 shillings; and one bolt, threepence." At the same time the purchase of "⅛ lb.

"These Terrible Men, The Harpes!"

Hyson Tea, 1s.10d," was recorded for the ladies' delicate palates.

On February 13, the wily Biegler adds "one lock for front jail door, 18s" to his already formidable armament. At the end of the month three pounds of nails, costing six shillings, "for the use of the jail," are purchased. And on March 7, a whole list of expenditures quite unprecedented in a turnkey's diary: "Hyson Tea, 1s.10d; 1 lb. sugar, 1s.6d; for the use of Susanna Harpe brought to bed by a daughter the preceding night: total, 3s.4d. Paid cash for midwife for ditto, 18s. Total: £1.1s.4d."

One more entry—and the most melancholy—in the jailer's cashbook, and Biegler's dealings with the Harpes were over. "March 16," he wrote. "For mending wall in the jail where the prisoners escaped, 12 shillings." His locks and handcuffs and horsebolts and nails had all proved futile. The Harpes were gone—leaving three women, now each delivered of a bouncing baby, to the jailer's tender ministrations.

But now the country was up in arms; excitement blazed; men, at the thrill of the man-hunt, seized rifles and plunged into the thicket. The law of "old Judge Lynch" was invoked: posses roamed everywhere in the wilderness, all armed with a length of

37

rope and eager to noose it around the murderers' throats.

One such party actually confronted the Harpes. Suddenly, as they waded through the forest, two men rose before them staring fiercely. There was a moment of startled hesitation, then both parties— the Harpes and the posse—went tearing through the thicket, in opposite directions!

Henry Scaggs, however, a famous "Kentucky Long Hunter" and a pioneer in 1770 with Colonel Knox, had been among the posse. Enraged, he tried to re-form the scattered party. But one look at the embattled Harpes had been enough to douse their enthusiasm; the man-hunters were bound for home.

Scaggs went on alone. An hour later he stumbled into a clearing and here he found a crowd of twenty or thirty settlers, jigging and drinking in the cabin of some newcomers, at the close of a "house-raising frolic."

Scaggs burst in among them with his dire news. The women clustered about him, screaming and exclaiming. The men, already half-full of whiskey, seized demijohns and rifles indiscriminately and plunged uproariously forth on the hunt.

Once in the forest, however, in the thicket already misting and darkening, their enthusiasm evaporated. Who were these Harpes, anyway? Again Scaggs saw his followers fade away. Again he went on alone.

"These Terrible Men, The Harpes!"

His way led him to the cabin of Colonel Trabue, another old Indian fighter and as hardy a veteran as himself. Trabue was willing enough to join the chase; only, he asked to wait until his son came home: the boy had gone down the trail to a neighbor's, to borrow some flour and beans. So the two men pulled their split-bottom chairs to the doorway; smoking and talking thus, they saw the boy's dog, all smeared with blood, come running home.

The dog led them back to the sinkhole where the youngster's body lay. Apparently the Harpes, famished and frenzied by the dangerous chase, had exploded in a very ecstasy of passion. Young Trabue had been shot, kicked, tomahawked, pummeled. His body was macerated by their blows, almost dismembered by their knives. Their whole booty had been a sack of beans and a bushel of flour. And again they had vanished. Trabue and Scaggs, though they hunted for days in the wilderness, found no trace of them whatever.

Meanwhile, back in Danville, the three women had come to trial. Their downcast looks, the hard condition of their life, the pitiful circumstances of their motherhood had all combined to sway public opinion in their favor. They were acquitted. They swore that now their only desire was to return to Knoxville and start a new life, so the settlers took

39

up a collection of provisions and clothing for them; some one added an old gray mare. And so, with the new-born children swung in a pair of hickory-withe panniers over the mare's back, they set out. The faithful Biegler accompanied them to the town limits: he watched them go trudging away, single file, into the wilderness. And there—though spies, on the chance that they might lead to the hiding place of the men, had been sent to trail them—they disappeared.

The spies traced them as far as the Green River crossing: here, they found, the women had traded their mare for a canoe, and vanished. No one can say now what motives impelled them—whether love, or loneliness; if that same mad fever the wilderness bred in the men's hearts had been communicated to theirs, or if it was only fear that drove them—all we know is that they loaded their children, provisions, clothing, into the canoe and paddled away. The gaunt Susan, Betsey, even the frail Sally Rice, the preacher's daughter, so soon accustomed to bloodshed—they were off to join their murderous masters at some preconcerted rendezvous.

Once again the Harpes had escaped, and pursuit had been checkmated. And now, while the country waited sullen and uncertain, news of two more murders traveled like thunder through the settlements.

A man named Dooley had been killed near the

"These Terrible Men, The Harpes!"

town of Edmonton. A man named Stump, a settler along the Barren River, was the other.

Stump's death had been pathetic. He had been fishing, it appeared, down the river; suddenly he noticed smoke, as from a camp-fire, rising above the trees on the opposite bank: he thought a party of new settlers had arrived. He sent a hail to them, over the water; then he rowed back to his own cabin: he slung a turkey and his string of fish over his shoulder, picked up his fiddle and a gallon jug of whiskey, and crossed to give the newcomers a proper welcome.

His body was found some days later: he had been tomahawked, disembowelled, his belly filled with gravel and his body flung in the river.

This news served at least to trace the passage of the murderers: they were apparently working north and westward, toward the Ohio and the Mississippi. It served also as a signal: as if a spark had been struck, the whole country flamed into activity. Doors that had been barred were opened; men poured forth to join the hunt.

Proclamations were posted. Rewards were offered, the State of Kentucky promising "a reward of THREE HUNDRED DOLLARS to any person who shall apprehend and deliver into the custody of the jailer of the Danville District the said MICA-

41

JAH HARP alias ROBERTS, and a like reward of THREE HUNDRED DOLLARS for apprehending and delivering as aforesaid, the said WILEY HARP alias ROBERTS, to be paid out of the Public Treasury agreeably to law. . . ."

At the same time, reliable descriptions were circulated: "MICAJAH HARP alias ROBERTS is about six feet high—of a robust make & is about 30 or 32 years of age. He has an ill-looking, downcast countenance, & his hair is black and short, but comes very much down his forehead. He is built very straight and is full fleshed in the face. When he went away he had on a striped nankeen coat, dark blue woollen stockings—leggins of drab cloth & trousers of the same as the coat.

"WILEY HARP alias ROBERTS is very meagre in his face, has short black hair but not quite so curly as his brother's; he looks older though really younger, and has likewise a downcast countenance. He had on a coat of the same stuff as his brother's, and had a drab surtout over the close-bodied one. His stockings were dark blue woollen ones, and his leggins of drab cloth. . . ."

Everywhere men were posted along the trails, riding through the thicket, hunting the elusive Harpes. Failing to find these—for their search failed—they turned their anger loose on lesser miscreants. The movement against the Harpes turned into a general clean-up of the whole territory.

Posses rode from town to town, tearing down grog-shops, burning bordels. Parties of Regulators linked forces through all the counties of Kentucky, hanging outlaws, horsewhipping and deporting. "Judge Lynch and Squire Birch" ruled the land. Fifteen people were hung; hundreds were whipped and driven away westward. Hundreds more escaped, fleeing ahead of their hunters, streaking west and north toward the Mississippi and the deserted regions along the Ohio.

When the great hunt finally ended and the posses disbanded, their satisfaction at the general clean-up of the settlements a little obscured the fact that in the purpose for which they had originally started they had been unsuccessful.

The Harpes were still abroad, uncaptured.

HARPES HEAD

WHILE thousands of immigrants were tramping over the Cumberlands and down the Wilderness Road, thousands more were coming in by water, down the Ohio. Pittsburgh marked the navigable head of the river and the town was thriving. Almost overnight it had swollen from a mere outpost to the size of a city: Wm. B. Irish, Esq., taking census at the beginning of the century, found 4,640 inhabitants housed in 767 buildings of which eleven, as he proudly specified, were built of stone!

Most of its population were either tavern-keepers or shipbuilders. Whiskey cost forty cents a gallon; brandy, eighty cents; beer, five dollars a barrel. In two years the town had launched twelve rigged ships, and barges, keelboats, broadhorns, Kentucky boats innumerable. Flatboats—"comfortable family boats well boarded up on the sides, and roofed to within seven or eight feet of the bow"—these sold for one dollar per foot of length: thirty to forty feet was the rule.

As fast as they could be knocked together the immigrants bought them. Haste made for carelessness; good wood lacking, rotten wood was used. "It behoves every purchaser of a Kentucky-boat to get it narrowly examined," warned Zadock Cramer but the immigrants were too anxious to be away: they would load in supplies—salt pork, flour, beans, potatoes, tea, sugar, an axe, cooking pots, powder and balls, some cutlery—and shove off down the bend.

The journey begun, however, many of them had occasion to regret their impetuous departure. The French, almost a century earlier, had called the Ohio "La Belle Rivière": even the captious Mrs. Trollope admired its beauty, remarking only that "were there occasionally a ruined abbey or feudal castle, to mix the romance of real life with that of nature, the Ohio would be perfect." But to the immigrants its winding course, its twisting channels, as well as the heavy forest wall that hedged each shore, were a source of constant menace.

Boats, snagged, sank and all on board were drowned or, what was worse, were set down unarmed and unprovisioned to wander starving in the wilderness. Indians flouring their faces to look like white men, Indians crawling on all-fours wrapped in bearhides tempted the travelers to land: landing, they were massacred. There was another danger even greater than the uncertain currents, or the bitter evasive Indians: bandits.

Thomas Ashe went down the river. "Most of the settlers on the lower parts of these waters are criminals either escaping from, or apprehensive of, public justice," he wrote. "I was warned that many of the small inns on the Kentucky shore were held in solitary situations by persons of infamous character. I demanded how a stranger was to distinguish a good from a vicious house." He was told to look to his landlord's ears: if they had been clipped or cut away entirely he might be sure that their owner had left them nailed to some market cross in the eastern colonies; by this indication, "a tolerable judgment of the host's character might be formed."

The towns, too—and especially along the lower reaches of the river—were populated by the same choice characters. Benjamin Van Cleve, floating down-river with a surveyor's party bound for Fort Massac, stopped over a day at the settlement of Red Bank.

It was a day of drizzling cloudy weather; the scattered cabins dripping dismally, the single street a churned mass of clay and mud: he found the town and its occupants alike disagreeable. "The place is a refuge, not for the oppressed, but for all the horse thieves, rogues and outlaws that have been able to effect their escape from justice in the neighboring states. Neither law nor gospel has been able to reach here as yet. A commission of the peace has been sent by Kentucky to one Mason"—ten years later Mason himself had turned bandit: his character had reversed completely—"and an effort has been made to introduce law; but the inhabitants drove the persons away and insisted on doing without.

"I inquired how they managed to marry, and was told that the parties agreed to take each other for husband and wife before their friends." Such an agreement was commonly held a sufficient contract in the settlements; sometimes couples so married would get their "Bible-wedding" later, when a circuit-rider appeared; in the wilder areas, naturally, this custom opened the way to many abuses. "I was shown two cabins with about the width of a street between them, where two men a short time ago had exchanged wives." Women were scarce in the early West.

From Red Bank on down to the town of Smithland, the river traversed its most dangerous section. Shoals abounded; sand bars lay just below the ripple of the surface; islands split the channel like a serpentine. Landsmen most of the river travelers were: as they came poling down, their jerry-built barges swinging awkwardly in the changing currents, they were helpless indeed to resist attack. A whole hierarchy of piracy had arisen, to prey on them.

The first of these had been a man named Wilson. At the head of the maze of snags and riffles known as the Hurricane Bars, some sixty miles below Red Bank, he took his stand at a cave in the bluff along-

47

shore: a cave like many others in those limestone regions, with deep chambers and hidden recesses and strange rock-formations. He posted a sign on the river bank: "Wilson's Liquor Vault & House for Entertainment." The cave was known as the "Cave Inn"—later twisted to "Cave-in-Rock." It had a long chapter in the history of river piracy.

Boat-wreckers waited along the bank: watching a boat pass, they would offer to pilot it through the channel. If the unskilled steersman chose to run the rip unaided, it was more than likely he would run aground: if he hired a pilot, the chance of his grounding became a certainty. Once beached, the boat and its occupants fell easily before the attack of Wilson's gang.

Sometimes the travelers would beach their boats of their own accord, planning to spend the night at the Cave and make the passage of the Bars in the morning. Next day, however, a different crew would man the barge, and a little more blood would have been spilt. Wilson had a sense of humor: he used to stand above the Cave, watching the flatboats drifting down to the ambush: "These people are taking their goods to market for me," he would say.

Wilson's sway was not undisputed; he had many rivals. One such was Colonel Fluger, known all through the West as "Colonel Plug," and renowned for his deviltry and his uproarious escapades.

Harpes Head

He became, finally, a legend among the boatmen: tales were told of his adventures, almost admiringly, wherever rivermen congregated. How he would "smouch" himself aboard a broadhorn, dig out the calking between the planks, bore through the craft's bottom; how, as the scuttled boat began to sink, his gang would come tearing in their skiffs to the rescue —a rescue that concerned only the goods aboard: the crew were left to drown.

How Pluggy's one obsession was his jealousy: he knew his wife's charms, and the weakness of his lieutenant, "Nine-Eyes," all too well. How, suspecting cuckoldry, he challenged Nine-Eyes to Gargantuan combat: armed with rifles, the two men took their positions; midway between them a bottle of prime Monongahela whiskey had been placed—the victor's prize.

They fired. Both were hit, but neither was too badly wounded to keep him from making for the whiskey. They met over the bottle.

"You air all grit!" said Plug.

"You waded in like a real Kentuck!" replied Nine-Eyes. And, share for share, they finished the bottle between them.

How, finally, Colonel Plug met the end to which he had committed so many of his victims: hid in the hold of a flatboat, boring away at the planking, he found the rotten material giving way too quickly; the boat, far out in midstream, sank too soon. Long before his followers, staging their rescue, could come aboard the vessel it had sunk. Colonel Plug, caught like a rat in his hiding-place, sank with it.

It happened, then, that when the great drive to clean up the territory and capture the Harpes began, the direction in which the fugitives fled was determined as much by what lay before them as by what menaced them in the rear.

Behind them, spread out in a great half-circle, the posses were sweeping them westward; ahead of them lay the lawless region of the Cave-in-Rock. When the hunt ended, the Cave was swarming with refugees and the lower Ohio a hive of outlaws. Drives and campaigns, we still have not quite learned, sometimes have paradoxical results: there is no doubt that by thus forcing the outlaws into mass formation the settlers themselves aided in the formation of the large bands of criminals—culminating in Murrel's enormous organization—which were later to prey on them.

The Harpes, however, were lone operators to the last. They came, with the other refugees, to the Cave; the three women had already rendezvoused there and were waiting for them. For a time they injected a new spirit, designed to interest the most blasé

Harpes Head

among the thugs, into the activities of the river pirates. They embellished the workaday business of boarding flatboats and murdering crews with bizarre and terrible refinements of torture.

"They seemed endowed with an inhuman ferocity. Neither avarice, want, nor any of the usual inducements to the commission of crime seemed to govern their conduct." In fact, they were homicidal maniacs, and the eerie quality of their actions, the strange shallow light their eyes reflected did not fail soon to set the outlaws' spines shivering queasily too.

Murder, in those dark regions, was an almost necessary concomitant of robbery. The traveler then broke all the links that bound him to past and future: he went into the wilderness as if into a temporary oblivion, from which no word or other warning of his passing might be expected to issue until he appeared again, at his destination. Such a man, met on the way by bandits and robbed only, might start forth into the settlements, to spread word of the attack. Kill him, and the gap between the beginning and the end of his journey remained forever unconnected, no one ever—or not for years— bothering to inquire what had become of him.

So these men had grown used to killing. But the Harpes made as it were an ecstasy of murder. A victim swiftly despatched represented to them a pleasure lost: they were like Indians; they preferred the

51

slow torture, the bloody anguish; they tore at men's bodies with knives and their bare hands, dismembering them. It was a little more than even the ruffians of the Cave could stomach.

One night—they had robbed a flatboat during the afternoon: two families moving down to settle on the lower waters had been massacred—the outlaws had gathered about the camp-fire on the beach, sorting the plunder. The Harpes, characteristically, were absent: greed was not one of their failings; they took what share was given them.

Suddenly, as the gang bent there, they heard wild cries, the thud of hoofs, a prodigious crashing from the thicket at the top of the cliff that rose behind them. They looked up, startled: it must have been a strange sight—against the black sky and the gray rock—the spectacle they beheld.

A great horse had plunged through the brush, leaping straight out over the lip of the precipice. Strapped to his back, stark naked and now wildly gesticulating, a man bestrode him. The robbers saw the ungodly apparition hang high above their heads a moment, the horse's neck outstretched, his legs still moving as if galloping; they saw the man lean over, his horrified face staring. Then horse and man came crashing down together, smashed in a bloody heap on the rocks along the beach.

While the outlaws sat stunned, the two Harpes

came scrambling down the cliff to join them, roaring with laughter. They had salvaged this victim from the crew of the flatboat; all afternoon they had saved him, to put on this show and surprise the boys.

Their idea of fun, however, had made the others a little dizzy. Such wit as this the cave-dwellers had never seen before, and they never wanted to see it again. They drove the Harpes—women, children, all of them—bodily out of camp. From then on the Harpes were outlawed even by the outlaws. All through the valley, every man had set his hand to destroy them.

Yet for over a year we see them, appearing and disappearing, like snakes in the underbrush striking and gliding away, murdering and tomahawking in an insatiable frenzy for blood—for over a year, before their last great chase begins.

We see them drifting down through Kentucky again. They need a rifle; the young son of Chesley Coffey, whom they meet along the trail, is carrying one. "Young Coffey was riding along a road one evening to get a fiddle. These terrible men smeared a tree with his brains, making out that his horse had run against the tree."

They weave back and forth. They move seemingly with inhuman speed; they strike with a terrible ferocity. No one can predict their actions. All any one can do is wait, and lock the doors until news comes that they are elsewhere. But they may be heading back again.

Two days after killing young Coffey, they murder William Ballard, in Tennessee near Knoxville. A week later they have moved north and west again. The women have been set down to wait for them somewhere in the wilderness: the two men are skirmishing alone. They encounter James Brassel and his brother Robert along the way.

And now a new stratagem has entered their crazy brains: constantly, henceforward, the Harpes will be asking news of the Harpes, pretending to be hunters on their trail. In the end, they seem actually to believe it: while the whole region is tracking them the Harpes, too, have joined the chase, hunting the Harpes.

So with the Brassel brothers. The four meet amiably, exchange gossip, ride along a little way together.

"We're lookin' for the Harpes," Big Harpe remarks, and they talk of the murderers' wild sorties. But in a little while his manner changes; his eyes narrow: "Now, I shouldn't be surprised if you was the Harpes yourselves, you two!" The Brassel boys begin to protest, but the others' guns are ready. "Ye say ye've just come from Barboursville? Well, we'll

"They make sugar from the 'sugar maple,' and coffee from the wild pea!"
—*A wood-cut from the Western Miscellany.*

"The Navigator, having now arrived after an irksome journey of between five and six weeks at the grand mart of business, the 'Alexandria of America, he leaps upon the shore with ecstasy, securing his boat to the shore with a careful tie, and mounts the Levee with elated heart."
—*New Orleans (from a print, dated about 1840).*

just ride back thar with ye and find out. Ye couldn't want fairer than that."

The elder of the two boys, confident that at the settlement he will be identified and freed, permits himself to be disarmed and trussed across his horse. Robert Brassel, moved by some sudden intuition, risks his life and escapes.

Stumbling panic-stricken along the trace, he encounters a party of men, all friends of his and all engaged in the eternal hunt for the Harpes. And by now the boy has guessed the identity of the two strangers; he tells his story; at a pounding gallop, the posse starts back up the trail.

They find his brother's body, the throat cut, the head battered, the gun smashed against a rock. Hardly pausing, the whole party rushes on, eager to capture the murderers.

But by now a kind of mystic terror embodies the Harpes. Even brave men quail from them. So with these men: sweeping forward, intent on vengeance, they see the Harpes, coming back!

Somewhere, in the interim, the women have rejoined them: perhaps they had merely lain hidden in the thicket by the roadside while the two men went about their bloody work. At any rate, there they all are, lowering and sullen-looking: the men, the three women and the children, loaded with arms and ammunition, moving forward in close formation, as if in battle array, along the trail.

Thus confronted, pursuers and pursued, they eye each other, and all the courage of the hunters ebbs away.

"Listen," some one suggests. "If they don't make no trouble let's us not start any." Silently, doggedly, the Harpes come on; they approach, pass abreast of the shrinking posse—"They looked very awful at them"—and move on down the trail. Still under the terror of their presence, the others are careful to continue up the trace for some distance, in the opposite direction, never speaking as they go, "so that nothing might be said that would be taken as a threat. . . ."

So through the spring and summer of 1798. Later —they have killed no one knows how many people in the meantime: John Tully, a farmer named Bradbury, the two Triswold brothers, John Graves and his son: they split their heads with an axe and threw them out in their own cabin yard, "where they lay until some one, seeing so many buzzards about, made an investigation and discovered what had taken place"; many others undoubtedly, in the lonely forest, were never discovered—later a directed purpose becomes apparent in the twisting path they have traced through the wilderness. They are looking for Colonel Trabue, seeking him to murder him.

Trabue, since the murder of his son by their hands, had already made himself their implacable enemy. Now that they are striking back at him, he makes what preparation he can, toward the event that he be murdered in the attack.

Being a Justice of the Peace, his preparation takes a legal form. He makes affidavit to their known crimes, together with a list of their victims. He prepares his own will. He draws up a description of the two Harpes and has printed copies of this distributed among the settlements:

"The big man is pale, dark, swarthy, bushy hair, had a reddish gunstock. The little man had a blackish gunstock, with a silver star with four straight points. They had short sailor's coats, very dirty, and grey greatcoats. . . ." Riders rush everywhere with the warning, crying, "Look out for the Harpes!"

Neighbors gather about Trabue's cabin. They watch the trails, filter cautiously through the forest. The old Indian hunter waits, his rifle ready.

But mad men are masters in the art of anti-climax. The settlers watch and wait—after how many false starts and sudden surprises—and watch again. The Harpes do not appear. They have forgotten Colonel Trabue and their vowed vengeance. They have struck west again, toward the Cave and the river country.

The Outlaw Years

They are moving up toward Red Bank again, no one suspecting them. John Slover, coming down the Highland Lick Road from a bear hunt, hears the click of a rifle's hammer behind him: he turns, sees the two men peering from the shrubbery, the gun that had missed fire still aimed at him; he escapes, but even now no one suspects their identity.

They pass through several settlements, bound on no one will ever know what terrible errand. Their women are no longer with them. Somewhere the two men have acquired fresh new suits, new black surtouts and buckskin gaiters. In this disguise, they represent themselves to be Methodist preachers, traveling to a distant congregation.

Arriving thus, they are welcomed at the cabin of James Tompkins, where the trail from Red Bank to Nashville crossed the Barrens of the Tradewater Creek. Tompkins invites them to share the noon dinner. They accept; Big Harpe, his great face owlishly solemn, says a long and unctuous grace over the food.

Tompkins marvels that two preachers should travel so heavily armed. "With such dreadful men as the Harpes abroad, my friend, it behooves us all to protect ourselves," Big Harpe replies. At this, the host remarks that he is in no condition for defense: he has scarcely any powder in the house.

Harpe, quite carried away by his sanctimonious

58

rôle, immediately pulls out his powder-horn and pours a cupful, gives it to Tompkins. They leave soon after, pausing in the saddle to invoke, with many "Amens!" from the Tompkins family, a blessing on the house.

Tompkins poured the powder they had given him into his powder-horn, loaded his rifle. A bullet from that rifle, propelled by that powder, was to knock Big Harpe from his horse and bring about his death, forty-eight hours later.

That evening, the night of July 20, 1799, the dogs began barking about the dooryard of Silas McBee's cabin. He opened his door. "Who's there?" he called. There was no answer. It had rained late that afternoon, and now the forest silence was filled with the drip of water among the leaves: it drowned all other sound. McBee waited, watching: he thought he saw the figures of two men lurking in the shadows along the road; thought he saw them make away, silently, among the trees. But he could not be sure. The dogs growled and bristled, then gradually quieted into their beds again. The farmer closed his door.

The Harpes had gone on, to the cabin of Moses Steigal who lived a mile or more down the road. They knocked, and here they were admitted.

There is a mystery in this connection. Steigal himself bore a dubious reputation in the settlement. That

The Outlaw Years

he knew the Harpes and had some under-cover relations with them appears certain. Of his own activities, little had ever been known, but he was a man of sudden disappearances, of long voyages to destinations only hinted at, of strange parleyings with furtive individuals: all these things, little noticed before, were to give rise to much comment later on.

He was absent on one of his journeys when the Harpes arrived, but he was expected home late that night and Mrs. Steigal was sitting up to wait for him. Besides herself, there was another person in the house: a Major William Love, a surveyor; he had called on a business errand and, finding Steigal gone, had climbed up to a bed in the loft, to take a nap until Steigal returned.

Though Mrs. Steigal knew the Harpes well, her husband had warned her never to betray their identity. So now the Harpes still held to their character of parsons, and when Love, awakened by the tramp of their arrival, came climbing sleepily down the ladder from the loft, Mrs. Steigal so introduced them. They all sat about for a while in the candle light, the woman sewing, the two Harpes chatting with Love: as always, they asked for news of the Harpes and spoke with horror of their deeds. Soon, Steigal still not returning, the men mounted to the loft together to take a nap.

In all probability, the Harpes had come to

Harpes Head

Steigal's for rest and concealment, and not with any murderous intent. But this man Love, lying unsuspecting between them on the straw-filled bedtick in the loft—Love, stretching and grunting and finally dropping off to sleep—the man was too great a temptation. Lying there, he was perhaps to their distorted passions as great an incitement as to the lover the sight of his mistress' hair spread tenderly across the pillow. Big Harpe's fingers itched toward his tomahawk.

A few minutes later the two brothers swung down the ladder from the loft-floor to the room below. Mrs. Steigal still sat with her sewing; Love had been killed while he slept without even a single awakening shriek but something—perhaps a spatter of blood on their hands, perhaps the glaring look of their eyes—told her what had happened.

"He snored so much!" growled Big Harpe, and started toward the shrinking woman. "What do ye mean by puttin' us in with a man that snored so?"

When Steigal came home, late that night, he found his house burning; he found his wife gasping, dying, and his baby, dead. The Harpes had gone on. Two more corpses showed the direction of their travel. Two neighbors named Gilmore and Hudgens had encountered them on the trail: Gilmore had been

61

shot dead; they had smashed Hudgens' skull with the butt of a gun.

Steigal—who had harbored them, who had protected them—now flamed into a rage as terrible as their own. The flare of the burning cabin in the dark night had attracted most of the nearby settlers —Squire McBee, Samuel Leiper, James Tompkins, John Williams—they stood wondering at the tragic happening, thinking how nearly this fate had been theirs. And now, galvanized by Steigal's frantic fury, they drummed up a posse among them on the spot and set forth, Steigal, implacable—"He was foaming"—in the lead.

They rode through the night and the day following, without sighting the fugitives. No one had brought much food—a little meal, a handful of jerked beef—they were hungry. They were about ready to turn back; they hadn't expected to be gone so long. Steigal held them to the chase. He would not give up.

So they camped that night, and rode on again, next day. Next day they sighted their quarry.

They sighted them far down across a valley, midway of the rise. Somewhere the Harpes had rejoined their women, and these now—the three women with their children—stood in a little cluster at the side of the trail. The two men had accosted a stranger along the way; they were talking, edging closer to him; undoubtedly they meant to kill him.

At the sound of the posse's coming, however, at the shots and cries from the heights, they abandoned their victim. The men leaped to their horses. Wiley rode straight for the thicket and vanished. Big Harpe spurred on down the trace: the hunt followed him. The women, even as the posse galloped shouting by —as if in some way they knew that the end had come —stood still as they had been standing, motionless, in a little cluster.

It was rolling country. The pursuers rode down one slope and up another; at the second hill top they had closed to within rifle range. Samuel Leiper was in the lead. He fired. The shot seemed to have no effect.

And when he tried to reload, he found his ramrod stuck in its casing: in the rainy weather the metal had rusted and jammed. He dropped his bridle; still galloping, he tried with both hands to free it. As he did so, Tompkins spurred up alongside him. "Here. Take my gun," he offered. "You got the fastest hoss and you are the best shot, so you better take it.

"And say!" he added, tapping the gun barrel. "I just recollected the charge of powder in there is from that feller's own horn! He give it to me day before yesterday. Now, seems like you ought to be able to hit him with that!"

Leiper did hit him. His next shot struck Big Harpe square in the spine. His pursuers saw his arms jerk wildly; with an effort he waved his tomahawk in one last flourish; his hand perhaps obeying some inner spasm of pain, he yanked his horse's head about and spurred straight for the thicket. The others, crashing blindly after him, followed.

When they emerged from the tangle of branches and briars, they saw Big Harpe again, now only a little distance ahead of them. He was rolling, dazed and almost unconscious, in his saddle; the horse, with a free bit, had slowed to a walk. Leiper and Tompkins had kept their lead on the rest of the party; now they rode alongside the bandit, pulled him from the saddle—he was too weak to resist—and sat down to wait for the rest of the party.

Steigal came riding in. In uncontrollable fury, he rushed to where Harpe lay. He kicked the dying robber; he waved his knife in Harpe's face. "I'm going to cut your head off with that!" he cried but the others restrained him: let the man die if he would, but if he lived they meant to bring him back to town to stand his trial.

Big Harpe breathed, stirred, stared about him. He asked for water. Young Williams gave him a little; he thanked the boy. The men sat about, resting after the long hard chase, staring at the man who had spread such terror. . . .

Big Harpe talked, from time to time, or tried to. His voice was weak: they could hardly understand him. He talked of his murders; he said he did not regret them; it became apparent that his mania had taken a religious turn: he said that "he had seen a vision, and the All-Wise had forged him for a scourge to humanity."

Big Harpe was slow in dying. He said there was one murder he regretted: in a fit of impatience at the child's crying he had snatched up his wife Susan's baby; he had "slung it by the heels against a large tree by the path-side . . . thrown it from him . . . into the woods." He regretted that.

So an hour passed, and Steigal was striding about, fuming and impatient: Big Harpe still lived. At last Steigal sat down near him. Carelessly, as if toying with the weapon, he pointed his rifle-barrel at Harpe's head. The dying bandit read his intention.

Slowly, painfully, he craned his neck, twisting his head, straining away from the deadly gun barrel. The muzzle of the rifle followed his movement. He jerked his head back the other way, faster. Steigal, still in the pale fury that possessed him, threw down the gun and laughed.

"All right!" he said. "I wouldn't shoot you in the

65

head anyway. I want that head. I told you I was going to cut it off."

He did cut off the head. "Stegall took Harp's own butcher knife, which Leiper had compelled him to deliver up, and taking Harp by the hair of the head, drew the knife slowly across the back of his neck, cutting to the bone; Harp staring him full in the face, with a grim and fiendish countenance, and exclaiming, 'You are a God Damned rough butcher, but cut on and be damned!'

"Stegall then passed the knife around his neck, cutting to the bone; and then wrung off his head, in the same manner a butcher would of a hog. . . ."

Steigal put Harpe's head in a bag they had brought, to carry it home with him: the trunk of the body they left to the birds.

A curious incident occurred on their return. They were now two days out from home; all their supplies had been eaten; they were hungry. And so, passing an outlying cabin, they were delighted to find that the farmer had plenty of roasting-ears of corn, and was willing to spare them some. They bought several dozen; Harpe's head, bloody and contorted, had been loaded in the only sack they carried, but that only bothered them a moment: with a shrug, they dumped the corn in with it. "He won't eat it!" they said.

And so, that night, they feasted—all except young

Harpes Head

Williams. "Young Williams would not eat any of the roasting-ears"—it struck them all as a piece of outlandish finicking—"and consequently he was forced to undergo the cravings of hunger until they returned to the settlements." Obviously, a young man a little too delicate for those hardy times.

So the two years of terror ended, though its reverberations still went occasionally rumbling through the wilderness country. Steigal, tasting vengeance, rode down the trace toward Red Bank, to the crossing at Robertson's Lick. Here, in the fork of a tree, he wedged Harpe's head and nailed it there. The spot is still called "Harpes Head," and for many years the skull hung there, rotted and rain-whitened, grinning down at the traveler.

One story tells that, in the end, an old woman took it down: her nephew had fits, and some conjuring doctor had told her that the one sure remedy was the bone of the human skull, pulverized and properly concocted. Whether the tale is true or not, no one knows: it would have been strangely fitting, certainly, had the head of the madman been pestled and powdered at last to such a crazy purpose.

Wiley Harpe—"Little Harpe"—had made good his escape, and five years were to pass before he reappeared. But the women remained, and upon them Steigal turned his hatred, still unappeased.

The Outlaw Years

They had been arrested; they came to trial, on no very definite charges. A court's decision, in those days, was often only the signal for the partisans of the contending parties to enforce their own. Steigal rode to the trial armed and surrounded by some of his mysterious friends, vowing to kill the women himself if they were acquitted.

In spite of their boasting, however, the Court ruled to acquit them. At the verdict, they were returned to jail again, under guard of the warden, Major William Stewart.

Stewart himself was a pioneer, and a fantastic character of the early days: "Often he appeared attired in an entire suit made of various 'lists' taken from the finest broadcloth sewed together, fantastically cut and fitted to his person, while the buttons on his coat and pantaloons were quarter dollars, United States coin, and his vest buttoned with genuine United States dimes." He remained an eccentric to the last. "On the morning of the day on which he died, he, with but little aid, drew on his curiously-constituted, many-colored suit of clothes, and in that attire he died and was buried."

But he could be grim on occasion, and Steigal probably knew as much. For a few days the strange avenger strutted and boasted; then, gradually, his enthusiasm cooled. His followers dispersed on more profitable errands; Steigal went home. In point of fact, the three Harpe women long outlived him.[1]

His conduct had not failed to arouse remark. His strange persistent vengefulness: grief for his wife seemed to have little part in it—he appeared to hate the Harpes for some other darker reason. His actions when the hunters caught up with their quarry: others of the posse told how he had been restless, almost like a man afraid—it was hinted that perhaps he had cut Big Harpe's throat to keep the man from talking, telling. . . .

A few months after he had ridden triumphantly into the settlement with Harpe's head slung in a bag across his saddle, Moses Steigal was himself in flight. With him traveled a young girl from a neighboring town: her name was Miss Maddox; they were eloping together.

They rode north, toward the river. After them came the girl's brother, intent on vengeance.

"Peak Fletcher and a brother of the young woman followed the runaways, and overtook them in the now State of Illinois." They found the pair lodged for the night at the cabin of one of Steigal's mysterious friends; silently, the two avengers approached.

---

[1] All three women, it is recorded, subsequently married and lived decorous and respectable lives. Morals, in relation to such matters as murder, etc., would appear to have been on the frontier largely the affair of circumstance.

The Outlaw Years

"Maddox and Fletcher fired upon Steigal through the chinks, and killed him." And they chose a gruesome moment for the shot: "Miss Maddox was sitting at the time in the lap of her lover, with an arm about his neck."

Aside from the steadiness of aim thus exhibited, there was another feature of the execution which many people mentioned with satisfaction at the time. The family honor had been cleared: it had been necessary to kill the seducer but the duty had been performed with commendable neatness and unobtrusiveness—"without," as a contemporary wrote approvingly, "doing any of the others any injury whatever."

II
HARE

"IT IS A DESPERATE LIFE"

MRS. FRANCES MILTON TROLLOPE visited New Orleans; she found "very little that can gratify the
eye of taste," although when she walked out with
her children to the forest at the edge of town and
saw the tall palmettos and the gay-colored paw-paw
trees, all hooked through with wild grape vines and
draped with the dim green of Spanish moss, her
prim little heart did stir at last: "It was our first
walk in the forests of the western world, and we felt
rather sublime and poetical."

But then, the whole day was full of novel sensa-
tions; coming back from their walk they stopped to
admire a hedge made of dwarf orange trees trained
together, and were greeted by a young negress working in the yard. "She was the first slave we had 'ever
spoken to, and I believe we all felt we could hardly
address her with sufficient gentleness. She answered
us civilly and gaily. . . ." It is possible the black
girl did not entirely fathom their clinical interest.

Robert Baird, on the other hand, received a quite
different impression: "This is one of the most wonderful places in the world!" he cried—he was speaking particularly of the river-ward face of the city.

73

"As far as the eye can see, almost, the margin is lined with flatboats. Some are laden with flour, others with corn, others with live stock, cattle, hogs, horses and mules. Some have traveling stores, some are to be found which are full of negroes, and some full of what is infinitely worse"—for Baird was a parson and a temperance advocate—" 'Old Monongahela Whiskey'."

So he turned his back on the river and strolled through the long arcaded alleys of the Market: "Such crowds! The busy and anxious-looking merchant. . . . Negresses and Quatre-Unes,[1] carrying on their bandanaed heads and with solemn pace a whole table—or platform as large as a table—covered with cakes, and apples, and oranges, and figs, and bananas, and pineapples, and cocoa nuts. . . ."

Thomas Ashe, as well, was struck by the brightness, the gaiety of the town, by—especially—the Creole damsels: "They are very beautiful. Their petticoats are ornamented at the bottom with gold lace or fringe richly tasseled; their slippers are composed of gold embroidery, and their stockings interwoven with the same metal, in so fanciful a manner, as to display the shape of the leg to the best advantage."

He sauntered under the China-trees whose shade

---

[1] An amusing bit of preciosity on the part of the reverend gentleman, who apparently tried to arrive at the etymology of the word "quadroon" by giving a French twist to its pronunciation. The derivation is from the Spanish "cuarteron"; the French say "quarteron."

made the gravel paths of the rue Marigny so pleasant a promenade. His long journey down the river was over; peacefully he dawdled in the cool gloom of the wine-cellars along Poydras Street, their walls tiered with bottles to the ceiling. No need, now, to study his landlord's ears; he turned his attention to the ladies'. "Their most general head-dress is either a handkerchief of gold-gauze braided in with diamonds, or else chains of gold and pearls, twisted in and out through a profusion of fine black hair. . . ."

Joseph Ingraham, more practical, admiring these barbaric beauties—"their lips are a blushing red, their bosoms are heaving snows"—remarked also that the gentlemen of the town carried heavy armament: the cane so daintily twirled by the dandy mincing down Chartres Street was a sword-cane; his short over-jacket, worn capewise with the sleeves knotted under one arm, concealed, more often than not, a dirk.

And the streets, to this observer, were "dark and noisome"; the coffee-shops were gay and colorful enough, but what pictured scenes were these that decorated the walls: "paintings . . . most of them of the most licentious description. . . !" It would seem that in this strange confusing city, half-Spanish, partly French, and now becoming American—in New Orleans each visitor found a different picture to describe.

The Outlaw Years

"Both the city and the suburbs are mere outlines, the greatest part of the houses being constructed of wood, having but one story, erected often on blocks and roofed with shingles; the whole being of a very combustible wood, that is, of cypress. There are a few houses, more solid and less exposed, on the banks of the River, and in the front streets. These houses are of burnt brick, having the upper part furnished with an open gallery, which surrounds the building. . . .

"In the winter, during the Carnaval, there is a public ball open twice a week. . . ." Berquin Duvallon, describing these balls, reveals that the hatred of the French settlers for their Spanish overlords had not died since those days in 1763 when by a stroke of the pen at the Treaty of Versailles the whole Louisiana Territory had come under the dominion of Spain and bands of rebel Frenchmen had roamed ragefully through the streets. He tells how even now the dances often ended in riotous disturbances, the men of the two races angrily confronting each other, the soldiers hurrying to quell the mêlée.

Thus once, in the midst of a reel, some gentlemen of the Governor-General's entourage appeared, resplendent in their uniforms. With the insolence of their caste, they stopped the music, ordered another more suitable to their tastes. But the public rebelled.

"It Is A Desperate Life"

"Contredanses françaises!" they yelled. *"A bas les espagnols! Nous sommes français!"*

The officers called their body-guard to aid them. Bayonets glistened in the doorways. Ladies screamed and fainted. Men drew swords. Duvallon's irony hints that the Yankee traders had already learned to profit by non-partisanship: "During this squabble and uproar, how did a number of Americans act, who were present at the ball?

"Men of a pacific nature and habituated to neutrality, they ran to the assistance of the fair ladies who had fainted away; and, loaded with their precious burdens, carried them off. Monsieur D...., a French merchant of the city, running to the succor of his wife, found her senseless in the arms of four Americans!"

Two decades earlier, Spain had demanded and the colonies had almost agreed to the astounding proposal to close the Mississippi completely against trade. There were military reasons for the demand. Spain held the western bank of the river from its unknown source to its mouth and here, in a narrow strip running eastward from a point just below Natchez to the Floridas, she held the eastern bank and the Caribbean coast as well.

She wanted no interference in her possessions and John Jay, accepting the proposal, and the Federal Government, almost ratifying it, appeared to agree

The Outlaw Years

with her. Only the new territories—Ohio, Kentucky, Tennessee—rebelled. For them, the River was the one profitable outlet of trade: how else—and certainly not by trekking their goods laboriously back across the Cumberlands—could they ever get their produce to the market? Kentucky, seeing its life menaced, threatened to secede, almost as soon as it had become a state. The whole Middle Valley protested. Washington reconsidered, refused to ratify.

Spain was forced, by reciprocal agreement, to admit the River as neutral water and countenance trade along its length. That trade, now, was the life of New Orleans. It brought cotton, peltry, lead, hemp and tobacco, molasses to fill the great stone warehouses back of the landing; it made the fortunes of the commission merchants; it sent the gold coins jingling across the counters of the banks.

It heightened the lights and it darkened the shadows of the city; it swept blanketed Indians, garlanded Creoles, trappers in buckskins and red-shirted flatboatmen, mulatto girls laughing—"money will always buy their caresses"—pig-tailed mariners and nigger slaves with jingling earrings—all in a slow swirl of kaleidoscopic color flowing past the flaring torches of the coffee stands that lined Poydras Street in the evenings.

It filled the town with glamor, with drunkenness, with gold, with murder, with romance. "The city

"It Is A Desperate Life"

abounds with tippling-houses, crowded day and night. All colors, white, yellow and black, mix indiscriminately. Such a motley crew, and incongruous scene!

"In this corner a party staking their whole cash at a game of 'All-Fours'; here slaves, free people of color of both sexes, and sailors in jacket and trowsers hopping and capering to the sound of a fiddle; there a party roaring out some dirty song. . . ."

It heightened men's wits and their passions. "Many stabbings are reported, and shootings; many people falling into the river from flatboat or levee and drowning, while drunk. . . ." It made a strange, bawdy, gaudy spectacle of life: a man, coming there, could enter it, let it take hold of him; no matter what his purpose, he could find its attainment there.

If he had no aim: if he were, perhaps, a young apprentice seaman jumping ship to see the sights of Chartres Street, then all the sooner would its brilliance penetrate him, find that dark gem, his soul, and set one facet gleaming.

Joseph Thompson Hare was born on a farm in Chester County, Pennsylvania, but he early moved to the cities. He was a hoodlum at heart, and the hard sharp crowded life of the cities sharpened and pinched him. New York, Philadelphia, Baltimore:

later, when he moved out across the dark soil of the wilderness, he remembered them hungrily.

He was sharp, but here was a land so wide that it made a bludgeon of the passions. He was quick, but quickness is an uneasy quality, in emptiness. In the end, he went back to the cities and to his death but meanwhile he made a name for himself in the western country—so great a name that even Murrel's best boast was, "I have robbed more than Hare ever did."

This model of his profession was a model in other ways as well. As a boy he had been apprenticed to a tailor, and the love of fine fabrics and flashy raiment remained with him to the end. A handsome lad, like Derry Dropper the legendary Beau Brummel of the wilderness highwaymen, he loved, like "Dandy Derry," a well-cut coat and a snug-fitting pair of breeches. Even when he tells of the capture that was to mean his hanging, he cannot resist including a few sartorial details: "I had bought one plaid coat, lined with crimson silk, at the price of $35, and one coat in the style of an officer's, at the price of $75, very dashy, when two men whom the owner of the shop had sent for, entered and apprehended us. . . ."

Liking to wear fine clothes, however, did not mean that he liked to cut them. He spent two years at the trade and learned it, then left beeswax and presser's goose behind him. He went down to the Battery and signed aboard a ship, to see the world. A month later he landed in New Orleans. When his ship sailed again, it sailed without him. He liked the town.

His sharp shrewd eyes soon saw that the city held a profit for him, too. These people from the up-country, these flatboatmen and planters were rough, raw, uproarious; they threw money around; they stuck their cash in their pockets: to this narrow-witted sharpster they seemed stupid, doltish. Soon he was picking their pockets in the cabarets, he was tripping them up in dark streets and plundering them, he was stealing through their unlocked doors and robbing them while they slept. He was cleaning up.

And with this success he began to lay bolder plans. He had seen the loaded boats come down the River; had seen the goods sold and the cash change hands. He had seen "every few days a company start from New Orleans on horses, and was told they carried a great deal of money with them through the Choctaw and Chickasaw Nations to get to Kentucky, Tennessee . . ."

He gathered his own companions about him, armed them and mounted them. He started up the trail, after his victims.

The Outlaw Years

Traffic down-river was, of course, made easy by the current; but, the trader once arrived in New Orleans and his goods sold, that same current defeated his return. Steam had not yet been more than dreamed of; some few travelers made their way up-river for short distances in small sailing-vessels or canoes but the majority—and especially those who came from more distant points, as Kentucky or Tennessee—traveled overland home again, with their cash, an uneasy burden, bound in their saddle bags behind them. There was but one road for them to go.

The trail led up the river to Natchez, and this far, through the Spanish territory, it was tolerably policed. Leaving Natchez, however, the road plunged straight through the wilderness, swamp-ridden, Indian-infested. "The road from Nashville to Natchez was estimated to be five hundred and fifty miles. The road was a mere trace or bridle-way through the woods and cane-brake." This road was the Natchez Trace. "Kentuckians and Tennesseeians took boats laden with produce down the river, which they sold at Natchez or New Orleans, and then returned to their homes by this route, carrying their money, which was sewn in raw hides. . . ." For years, the Natchez Trace had a bloody history—of robbery, of ambush, of murder—as the bandits prowled there.

82

"It Is A Desperate Life"

John L. Swaney traveled the Trace, but with a different purpose than such men as Hare. Toward the close of the century, a Government mail route had been established, linking the American settlements and the Spanish province: from 1796 until about 1810 he was one of its messengers. His memoirs give a graphic picture of the conditions at the time.

The mail consisted of "a few letters and government dispatches, with a few newspapers": beside his mail-pouch, he carried "one-half bushel of corn for his horse, provender for himself, an overcoat or a blanket, and a tin trumpet." It took him ten days for the trip to Natchez.

"He would leave Nashville on Saturday night at eight o'clock"; he would go clattering down Market Street from William Tab's store where the post-office was located, and so out through the cabins of the town, already darkened for the night.

Toward midnight, he would reach the Big Branch of the Harpeth River: here lay Tom Davis' cabin and clearing. Davis' dogs would bark at his galloping passing; Swaney would answer with a hailing cry. This was the last white man's dwelling: beyond lay the wilderness.

"Sunday morning he would get to Gordon's Ferry on the Duck River, 51 miles from Nashville, which was then the line between Tennessee and the Choc-

taw Nation. There he fed his horse and ate breakfast.

"He had then to ride 80 miles to Colbert's Ferry,
on the Tennessee River, before night set in, where
the Indians would set him across." This was a hard
day's riding, after a night in the saddle, but he had
to make it. "The Indians were contrary, and would
not come across the river for him if he failed to get
to the landing before bed-time."

This ferry was operated under the auspices of
old James Colbert, chief of the Chickasaws; on the
opposite shore they maintained a kind of inn, where
Swaney stayed the night. It afforded the rudest kind
of shelter, and its hospitality was colored by native
superstition. Mrs. Thomas Martin, following the
Trace, spent a night there and described it: the Indians were very agreeable to them—gave them a supper of venison, potatoes and coffee, while "Mrs. Colbert," wife of the old chieftain, paraded about, wearing a Paris hat, but barefoot—but would not let
them sleep in the house: "They assigned us to another, where slept not less than fifty Indians, many
of them drunk, while my husband and others sat
up all night. It is not their custom to let strangers
sleep in the house with their families."

Leaving here, Swaney pushed on deeper into the
wilderness: "He would have to go to the Chickasaw Agency, 120 miles, before he would see a house,

or even an Indian wigwam, and would have to lie
out one night in the woods or cane brake. . . ."

At the Chickasaw Agency he encountered the first
white men since leaving Nashville. Even these were,
in a certain sense, outlaws. "The Chickasaw Agency
was kept by McGee, who was the agent, with Jim
Allen as interpreter. Allen was a man of fine address, and was a lawyer who came from Nashville,
but failing in business, went off among the Indians. . . ."

Two hundred miles farther on lay the Choctaw
Agency: "The route was entirely through Indian
country": compared to this, the first half of the
journey had been populous. One hundred miles farther still, and he entered Natchez.

It was here, in this three hundred mile wide strip
of canebrake, swamp and desolation ruled by the
Chickasaws and Choctaws, that the danger to travelers lay. The danger was not in the Indians, or
rarely. Occasionally a wandering band of Creeks—
"great warriors"—cut. through the land, but the
others were "kind and peaceable. The Chickasaws
always boasted that they had never shed the blood
of a white man in anger. Allen often told Mr. Swaney that the Chickasaws and Choctaws were the hap-
piest and best people he had ever known. They could
not say anything in their native tongue worse than
'skena' (bad) and 'pulla' (mean) and in all his

85

knowledge he never heard of the crime of adultery being committed but once. The punishment in such a case was to cut off the end of the nose of the woman. . . .

Happy Jim Allen! He had lived but a year among these pleasant savages, when his eye grew desirous of one of their virtuous maidens. "The manner of choosing a wife among the Chickasaw Indians was for the swain to make his desire toward a particular maiden known to the chief, and having gained his consent, the suitor would return to his wigwam and there wait until his lady love should be sent to him."

In Allen's case the matter had certain complications: his choice had fallen upon no less a person than Susie, daughter of the chief, James Colbert himself. Many braves had been her suitors. Allen, however, paid formal visit to the potentate, made his plea. He then, as custom demanded, retired to his wigwam, closed its flaps and waited there in the darkness while the elders of the tribe debated his request.

"He waited until nearly dark, when Susie Colbert made her appearance at his door with a blanket drawn closely around her head, leaving only space enough for her to find her way, and in response to his invitation, walked in and took a seat. This was Jim Allen's courtship and marriage."

The union thus formed was fruitful, of a daugh-

"It Is A Desperate Life"

ter: her name was Peggy Allen. In Swaney's time she had grown into young girlhood: he reported that she was "the prettiest woman he ever saw," and in those days, in the womanless West the fame of a lovely girl spread all through the territory: men would come traveling hundreds of miles, like zealots on a pilgrimage, to settle their longings and look upon her. "Mr. Swaney said it was almost incredible the number of travelers and boatmen who stopped at the Agency to see her, attracted alone by her reputation. She was known to all the boatmen as a great beauty."

But she was wilful. Allen's brother, a substantial man, came out from North Carolina to visit them; he tried to persuade Peggy to come east with him; he offered to school her, and launch her out as a belle in eastern society. She refused.

Sam Mitchell, the agent in the Choctaw territory, fell madly in love with her. He found no favor with her but he did gain the support of her grandmother, old Chief Colbert's wife. With craft, this beldame invited the girl to visit her in the Indian encampments: she immediately dispatched her, perforce, to Mitchell's cabin, "with eight or ten negroes and as many ponies as dowry."

Here was danger of an involuntary bridal, but Peg still showed her spirit. She told Sam Mitchell "she would never marry a drunken white man or an Indian"; she locked the doors of the man's own cabin against him. Baffled, after two weeks Mitchell sent her home again.

Allen was proud, but he was also sensible. They were alone in the wilderness. If Mitchell chose to seek vengeance through his Choctaws they had no defense among the Chickasaws: in fact his greater fear was that Grandma Colbert, more spiteful still, might be moved to savage reprisals.

But Peggy had another suitor, young Simon Burney, the son of a Natchez planter. She had dallied Simon for years but now, in the uncertainty, she grew more lenient toward him. "He would almost give his life for you," her father told her.

So they were married; Peg was whisked downriver to Natchez, away from the dark threat the wilderness had conjured to oppose her beauty. They settled at Natchez; their fate was happy: "Birney amassed a large fortune, and raised and educated a nice family."

The boatmen and the travelers loitered no more at the Agency, feeding on Peggy's loveliness. Those who came, passed hurriedly. For now there was danger along the way.

Hare, with his three companions, had begun to levy on the Trace. They jogged northward pleasantly, taking their time, looking about them; they found the prospect agreeable: it was a vacation from the city. And the region abounded in game: wild turkey, deer, raccoon—every night their campfire menu boasted delicacies that the grill rooms along St. Charles Street might have featured.

Moreover, they found the venture more profitable than they had hoped. Hardly beyond Natchez, just entering Indian territory, they had overtaken a party of travelers; the surprise had been complete.

"Lord bless my soul!" said one of the plucked wayfarers, as Hare reached for their saddle-bags, and the bandit knew he had uncovered rich treasure.

"We took three hundred doubloons, 74 pieces of different sizes and a large quantity of gold in bars, six inches in length and eight square—thirty-weight of it. With the others, I found 700 doubloons and five silver dollars, and four hundred French guineas, and 67 pieces the value of which I could not tell until I weighed them. I got twelve or thirteen thousand dollars altogether from the company, all in gold."

The robbers had adopted the expedient of painting their faces with berry-juices and bark stains, like the Indians going to war. It served as an excellent disguise; moreover, the weird coloring heightened the terror of their aspect.

"One of the men looked very blank at seeing all his money taken from him, and swore he'd be

89

damned if he did not deserve better luck, 'for he had got it after an hour and a half's hard fighting!' He told me he had been on board a privateer, and seen some danger, but he could not fight without a noise, and this damned place was so quiet and mournful, he felt as if he were going to the devil every moment.

"I told him I would stand his friend, and gave him his watch and several gold pieces, and he looked as thankful as if I had done him a favor, instead of robbing him. . . ."

Hare and his men pushed on into the wilderness, casting about for a hide-away headquarters safe against attack. They found it soon, up near the northern limit of the Chickasaw country, just under the Tennessee line.

"We came across a spot that seemed a very good retreat, and a very comfortable home too. It was on one side of a cane brake, where the cane grew very thick and tall, and would have concealed us from the best eyes. These cane brakes are very much frequented by wild animals of all sorts, especially wildcats, and are kept clear of generally. Our habitation was in a cleft rock, where one rock jutted very much over another, and made a sort of cave, that we could easily make safe from every savage that walked the wild wilderness. We had a good feather bed in our cave."

"It Is A Desperate Life"

As it turned out, however, they had little cause to fear the savages; to the Indian, tracking the wilderness, outlaw and merchant-traveler were alike. Soon Hare and his men were trafficking in the encampments, buying parched corn and meal and tobacco from the squaws: an old brave known as "Hay-Foot" acted as their scout along the trail.

Hare's danger was more insidious than the armed attack: it lay in the silence that his ears strained at, in the loneliness that twisted his very bowels with bewildered foreboding. Hare was a man of imagination: moved by this emptiness, this lack of everything his cramped soul had grown used to, the writing of his diary assumes a real descriptive power.

The first night they camped at the cave, the subtle attack of the wilderness began. Sprawled in a row on the feather bed, his companions snored comfortably but Hare lay awake, with that chill damp, that sick sense of the futile passage of time which sleepless men know. "As for me, I could not sleep, but lay looking, sometimes in the fire which I had kindled, and sometimes at the stars, and listening to the wind in among the cane brake, which made such a mournful rustling sound. . . ."

And a few days later: "We came across a company of four men. I had hard work to save their lives. We stopped them: we had hid all the horses from the sight of the road. I stepped up to the one that had holsters before him, and told him that I had twelve highway robbers under my command, and the first man that moved should be blown to hell. The dry cane made a great crackling: it was so thick in that spot that a man could not be seen ten feet from the road.

"It was a cloudy day, and everything looked black and gloomy, and the sound of the cane, though it did not frighten me, made me feel very strange and out of the way. . . ."

So for a moment he hesitated: the very air seemed to quiver with apprehension and Hare was staring numbly at the little band of travelers he had halted: their white faces, their eyes glistening with fear.

Behind the thicket, his men were muttering; one of them stepped out on the path and approached Hare: "Shoot them and have done with it," he said.

At this one of the merchants—he was an oldish man—began to shake. "For God's sake . . . for God's sake!" he kept repeating.

But the robbers cried out from their hiding place that they were not disguised and if he let the men live they should all be arrested and recognized later. Immediately the travelers, made earnest by their terror, protested and promised roundly never to speak of them, never to describe them to a soul.

"I told them it was well thought of, and further that if there should but one man move till I gave

the signal they would all be landed in eternity; and
with this I called to one of my companions to come
up and take their money." Seven thousand dollars
was the total of the haul. They were growing rich.

But Hare had become a difficult man to live with;
his moods jumped and jerked and varied. He would
lie sleepless at night; he would ride out alone by
day. He had imagination enough to sense his peril,
but not enough comprehension to plumb its sources:
all he knew was that the silence irked him; that
the tiny cracklings, the soft whisperings that lurked
in the center of that silence irritated him more.

One adventure at this time was near being the
end of him. He encountered a slave trader from
Natchez. "I was by myself, and had left the men
at the cave. I had one pistol with me, and felt a
desire to do something by myself." So he pounced on
the returning slaver. It was a foolish thing to do.

"I rode up on his left side, and told him to deliver his money, for I was the devil, and would take
him to hell in a second if he did not drop that
gun off his shoulder, and his pistols too, if he had
any." But Hare had been too careless; he had not
even drawn his weapon. And the trader glanced
back, saw that he had but one man to deal with, and
decided to take a chance.

As if in obedience to the command, he let the gun

slip from his shoulder; as the muzzle swept down, he pulled the trigger. The charge flared in Hare's very face; his hat was blown off; his horse leaped frantically.

Jerking at the reins, Hare whipped out his pistol. But the smoke from the other's musket had been so dense that he had to fire blindly: he could not see his man. As he pulled trigger he noticed two men, on horseback, halted a little way along the trace; one had a rifle at his shoulder.

It was a ticklish moment. The smoke drifted. "I had not hurt the trader in the least, but he looked frightened, and I told him to clear himself as fast as he could be off, or I would give him another fire." As the man galloped away, Hare calmly dismounted to recover his hat, reloaded, and waited for the two strangers to come up.

We of the well-protected present find it difficult to animate the figures that populate our picture of those early days: we see them in tableau, or rather as if frozen immobile in a single characteristic pose, like the statues grouped in a monument to the pioneers.

We see the woodsman with ax upraised; we see the Kentucky-boatman leaning to his oar; we see the mounted traveler along the path; we see the highwayman, pistol in hand, crouched peering in the .canebrake. But when, for a single moment in their lives, we can trace their deeds and set them moving they pass, in the instant, beyond our comprehension.

The ax falls, to a rhythm different than we had expected. The boatman's lips give forth a chantey, and though the words are familiar to us his intonation invests them with a strange foreign significance. The highwayman and the traveler meet and clash in the wilderness but the fear of one, the bravado of the other find outlet in actions quite beyond our understanding.

So with Hare. He waited; the two travelers drew up and halted abreast of him. They had a sly, cozening look in their eyes.

"Seen any deer hereabouts?" drawled one.

Hare said that he had, indeed.

"I suppose that was one ye fired at just now?" the questioner went on. "Why didn't ye kill it?"

"A man sometimes will miss a thing," was Hare's answer.

The two men stared at the robber, grinning: it was as if the escapade with the trader—the fuddled shooting into the smoke, the hats blown off, the frightened galloping—had been a little secret joke between them. At last they picked up their reins and jogged away down the trace. When they had gone a little distance Hare heard them burst into loud guffaws of merriment.

The Outlaw Years

Their profits so far had been considerable; they had been three months in the wilderness: it was time to begin spending. "I must get back to a town and enjoy myself," Hare decided. By common consent they headed north, for Nashville.

They lodged at "a very good house, kept by a widow lady"; they lived very well. The men drank and had many fights. Hare himself took rather the fancy to make himself a gentleman: he bought "a black boy, and two horses and a gig." Later, riding and driving together, they all set out for Louisville.

Here they sold the gig; they took passage in a flatboat and drifted down the river to Natchez, and from there to New Orleans.

So they found themselves back in the gay glittering town again. "Here we staid seven months, and put up at a house kept by an Irishman from New York, who kept a great tavern and was a great sport. Twice a week a great many respectable persons met at his house to play at dice, cards and billiards, and a curious game called the 'United Stabel,' with 32 figures on it, of different colors. I and my highwaymen lost a great deal of money by playing at this table."

Their funds were still further depleted by the unreasonable demands of a certain French gentleman, a fellow lodger at the Irishman's, who had discovered one of Hare's light-fingered companions delving into his strong-box. They finally had to pay the fellow "thirteen hundred dollars, to make him hold his tongue."

Soon after—money gone, credit gone—they set out for the Trace again. This time they had learned another trick: they had procured passports from the unsuspecting Spanish authorities. Now, if threatened on American soil, they could take refuge as citizens in Louisiana.

To be nearer the border, they made their headquarters just north of Natchez, camping in a cave which, as Hare lugubriously speculated, "no man had ever visited before, I expect, since the flood." And again the impassive wilderness surrounded him; its silence gripped him. It was a gloomy spot they had chosen: "There were a great many swamps in the neighborhood, filled with Alligators, very large, and that made a great noise. Sometimes they cried like a young child. They are very ugly creatures. . . ."

Hare began to write his diary. Almost the first words he set down were: "Let not any one be induced to turn highwayman by reading this book and seeing the great sums of money I have robbed, for it is a desperate life, full of danger, and sooner or later ends at the gallows."

The Outlaw Years

Two months, and they were back in town again, sipping the wines of Mme. Saluces, smoking their long-stemmed pipes, flicking flowers at the feet of passing girls. They took the baths at the Bayou Saint-John and lunched at the fish-grills along the Shell Road. They hired their gig of a Saturday afternoon and drove down to Lake Saint-Charles, already a rendezvous for sporting gentlemen and sporty ladies as well.

Hare loved the city: he loved the smell of trampled fruit in the market place, the rattling sound of feet along the plank sidewalks, the intricate lacy pattern of the moving populace. And now, with the shadow of the wilderness always behind it, the city danced before his eyes like a mirage; he snatched at everything; he was afraid it would vanish at his touch.

And yet there was still a queer resentful flavor in his mood. All his pleasures were bitter ones; life had become a sullen affair. Drinking led to fighting: Hare was a battler when aroused: he whipped Bill Marshall the bully of the river-flats; shortly after, he was fighting one of his own gang.

This was a lad who had found a way to turn his good looks to account: he made a business of marrying young girls and decamping with the dowry. He had left a trail of widows up and down the River. But now, when he turned up one day with a tender

"It Is A Desperate Life"

little Spanish girl, fresh from a nunnery in Bâton Rouge, Hare's anger flared. This was a wrong thing to do, he argued; "I told him he would get no good from this." He preached at the unlucky fellow: ordered him to return the girl to her parents.

Perhaps the other saw an inconsistency in his leader's position. He made no answer, seemed to agree: next morning he and his wife were gone, and so was Hare's wallet containing seven hundred dollars.

Hare came up with him a few days later. "I met him at a tavern where he was boasting of being able to whip any man in town. I thought this a good opportunity to take my satisfaction out of him." The challenge was passed and accepted. The two men, followed by a crowd of hangers-on, adjourned to a large field outside the town. "I gave him as handsome a dressing as any man ever got."

And those were bloody battles they fought in those days. The gambler Devol, himself a mighty bruiser, tells of a fight he had on a river-boat: "When we got on deck, the mate made a ring with some barrels and said, 'No man but the fighters shall get inside the ring.' The big fellow stripped down to his undershirt, and looked like a young Samson; then the bets ran up to $100 to $25. I pulled off my coat and vest and stepped into the ring. He made a lunge: I dropped my head and he hit it a terrific blow.

99

Then he got one in below the belt, and I thought for an instant I would lose my supper and the fight; but I rallied, and got a good one on the side of his neck, which doubled him up like a jack-knife; then I ran in, caught him, and let drive with my head. I struck him between the eyes, and he fell over as if he had been shot. . . ."

So, scrambling, gouging, tripping, kicking in the groin, butting in the belly, Hare fought for the honor of the deluded Spanish maiden. "Every time I caught hold of him he bellowed for help. He was like a wolf caught in a sharp trap. I whipt him until he hollowed, 'Enough!'"

When it was over, the beaten bridegroom lay senseless, bloody. They thought he had been killed. Hare and his two companions ran to cover at Pensacola.

This small town was a military outpost; there were rumors of war afloat: the town was feverishly gay. Hare and his men lodged at "a very pleasant boarding-house kept by a widow named Madame Valery." They were soon sparking about the town as flauntingly as ever.

"One day one of the boarders asked me if I had heard the news. I was alarmed"—he thought it might have to do with the murder he thought he had committed—"but it was only that I and my companions were picked out to give the next ball, on

that night week." It was the custom then for gentlemen of the town to alternate in sponsoring a cotillon.

Hare and his men took their turn with the rest. It
cost them three hundred dollars, but they invited
everybody: "I was much pleased to find the Spaniards so agreeable. They were full of mirth. We
danced the fandango with a fiddle and tambourine."

The ball, as it turned out, had a fortunate after-
math. Later, leaving Spanish soil, they were seized
at the border. Spain, England, France and the
United States were all at odds. A squadron of gun-
boats lay at Bâton Rouge; Governor Claiborne of
Mississippi had troops ready to send into Florida;
New York papers were remarking that the Spanish
colonies were "evidently destined to become an in-
tegral part of the United States"; Tennessee, through
its Legislature, pronounced itself "ready to support
such honorable measures" as might be needed, in the
event that "the United States are involved with one
of the belligerent nations."

Hare and his fellows showed their passports. They
were disregarded. It was charged that they were
American spies; they were clapped into jail. In the
emergency, they had recourse to their friends at
Pensacola. At the appeal, the whole list of guests
at their cotillon responded, testifying to their character, their amiability and honesty. They were freed.

The Outlaw Years

But Hare had begun straining to propitiate his fate. As he had fought with one of his companions to keep him in the straight monogamous path, so now, as they rode north for the Trace, he argued with the others: "I read them from John Wesley's magazine." He preached at them to abandon the life of the highwayman.

Like many another evangelist his concern was more with the souls of others than with his own. And yet his own spirit had felt the bite of the wilderness. They rode northward; they took some ten thousand dollars while Hare sulked and proselytized. "We raked the woods from the Southwest Point to the Choctaw Nation"; and here, at the Tennessee Line, the companions separated forever.

Hare, with a dismayed mind, with his soul shivering in the darkness his life had run upon, rode on toward Nashville. It was a clear night, a starlit night, when his doom focussed him.

He had robbed a drover that afternoon; had taken the man's pistols and a small sum of money. "About nine o'clock, the night I robbed the drover, as I was riding along very rapidly to get out of the reach of pursuit, I saw standing right across the road, a beautiful white horse, as white as snow; his ears stood straight forward and his figure was very beautiful.

"When I approached him, and got within six feet

"When the traders stopped at night they would hide their money in the woods some distance from the camp before they would make a fire, to prevent being robbed."

—From the Western Miscellany.

"Even decent, quiet deacons at home would throw aside religion and peace when they embarked on their annual trip down-river."—A print from "A History of Travel in America", by Seymour Dunbar. Copyright 1915. Used by special permission of the publishers, The Bobbs-Merrill Co.

of him, he disappeared in an instant, which made me very uneasy, and made me stop and stay at a house near there, all night."

That delay was his fatal error. He had hardly reached his bed when a posse, led by the mulcted drover, overtook him. The house was surrounded; Hare was taken. He served five years in jail, reading the Bible and writing in his Confessions. When released, he fled the wilderness; he had been warned: "I think this white horse was Christ," he said, "and that he came to warn me of my sins, and to make me fear and repent."

A year after his release, on March 12, 1818, the night mail coach from Baltimore was held up near Havre-de-Grace. Hare engineered the job. The loot was $16,900.

As the robbers prepared to go, one of the passengers whom they had left tied to a wagon wheel begged that his watch—it was an heirloom—be returned to him. Hare held his lantern high to look for the time-piece; its light revealed his face. Two days later, as he debated between the plaid coat and the coat of crimson silk in a Baltimore tailor's shop, the same passenger entered and identified him.

The case was speedily brought to trial. Identification was absolute; the death penalty seemed certain. But Charles Mitchell, Hare's lawyer, had found a loophole in the law: at the arraignment, he advised his client to stand mute, on the question of his plea. This action brought forward a question which, in the inchoate legal condition of the day, had never been developed before.

Robbing the mail was a crime against the Government. An Act of Congress, previously passed, had propounded that if a prisoner stood mute when asked to plead, it should be taken that he had pleaded guilty. This Act, however, was specifically enforceable only in the case of treason and other capital crimes against the Government.

Now, at the time of the passage of this Act, robbing the mail had not been made a capital crime. A later Act of Congress had included it in the category of crimes punishable by death, but the shrewd Mitchell argued that since the second Act had not been retroactive, the provisions of the first Act did not apply, and consequently if his client stood mute at the pleading, no plea could legally be taken. Ergo, no trial could be had.

There were witnesses, evidence, testimony ready, but it began to look as if in face of it all, if Hare could keep still long enough, the Court would be forced automatically to turn him loose.

In the emergency—but only after a long wrangle of several months' duration had beguiled the lawyers—the Court handed down an opinion: if a prisoner stand mute, his position amounts to a constructive confession, implying the plea of guilty. At the same time, the prosecution unearthed an old law of the State of Maryland, providing that in grave offenses, if the prisoner stand mute, the Court shall proceed as if on a plea of not guilty.

Thus, where there had been no plea at all, the Court now found itself provided with two: it could proceed as if the still silent Hare had pled either guilty or not guilty. Once the machinery of justice got in motion, as it developed, it made little difference which choice was taken. The trial that had taken four months to begin, took four days to conclude.

On Thursday morning, September 10, 1818, Joseph Thompson Hare was led from his cell into the prison yard at Baltimore. A delay of about an hour ensued, occupied with the preparation of the gallows-trap: a concourse of about fifteen hundred people waited patiently; Hare spent the hour praying and reading his Bible. He was hanged shortly after ten o'clock.

III

SAMUEL MASON

ONE OF THE BOLDEST SOLDIERS

AND still the boats came booming down the River. It was no longer only the makeshift craft of the emigrant that one saw upon the waters: the River had become a highway for trade, for freight and passenger traffic.

Scows, batteaus, arks with pointed stem; Kentucky-boats and flatboats roofed over and decked, broadhorns, so called for the two great "gouge-oars" projecting one on either side of the bow; rafts and barges: laden with "hoop-pole and punkins," produce and trade-goods, they came poking down the reaches and around the bends.

The keelboat had been developed for upriver traffic as well as down. Heavily built, with a keel of four-inch timber along her bottom and a stumpy mast in the bow, she could sail before the wind; if the wind failed a long line called the "cordelle" was fastened to her mast-head and carried ashore where a crew of thirty or forty men towed her while twenty men more, in endless chain on a runway along her sides, aided with poles.

Out of the keelboat grew the Ohio packet-boat, larger and more unwieldy still, one hundred feet long and twenty wide, with a cargo box forward and a passenger cabin aft: even with eighty men poling and towing, it took such a boat a month to make the run from Cincinnati to Pittsburgh and return.

If slow, they were at least safe; the large crews were all, as the early advertisements took care to specify, "very skillful in the use of weapons"; some of the packets were armed with small cannon as well.

The crews were hard, rough, "a rude and lawless class of men": their life made them so. "I am a man. I am a horse. I am a team. I am an alligator. I can whip any man in all Kentucky, by God!" was their boast. In summer they worked stripped to the waist, tanned coffee-brown; in the cold winter they wrapped themselves, grotesque as Indians, in furs and blankets and heaved against the poles.

They slept on deck; they ate on deck, with a pan full of bread and meat set down among them, and a "fillie" of raw Monongahela whiskey to wash it down. "Much of the distance through which they traveled in their voyages was entire wilderness": they must be prepared to fight Indians or pirates at any moment.

Indians failing, they fought among themselves. The champion of each boat-crew stuck a red turkey feather in his cap: placed there, it was a challenge to any other bully on the River.

Lacking other opponents, they fell upon the

One of the Boldest Soldiers

townspeople. Sober citizens in the River settlements dreaded their arrival. "Each keelboat carried from thirty to forty boatmen, and a number of these boats frequently sailed in company. The arrival of such a squadron at a small town, was the certain forerunner of a riot. . . ."

Mike Fink was the hero and champion of them all: his name grew into legend; the tales of his marvelous doings passed into fantasy.

Mike Fink was a marvelous shot with the rifle. All down the River whenever a shooting contest was held and a quartered steer put up for prize, by common consent Mike Fink, without firing a shot, was awarded the "fifth quarter"—the hide and tallow. He could drive nails with bullets. Once, when the boats were tied to a landing, Mike sighted a nigger standing along the bank: the fellow's feet were so flat that his heels stuck out in a knob behind. Instantly, Mike drew a bead on the excrescence and shot it off. "The fellow couldn't wear a genteel boot with his foot like that," he stated, "and I wanted to fix it so he could."

Mike Fink was a great drinker. It was a sober day for him when he didn't drink his gallon of whiskey and more. No human man was ever able to keep track of how much he needed to get himself a real roaring drunk.

Mike Fink was a joker. Strolling ashore one day,

he noted a fine flock of sheep grazing in a farmer's meadow. He took a pair of them and rubbed snuff in their snouts; then he called the farmer, pointed to the snorting pawing animals.

"What's the matter with them?" asked the simple farmer.

Mike Fink said: "They've got the black murrain. If you don't shoot them the whole flock will get it too."

That was the occasion for a fine feast aboard the flatboat, for Mike magnanimously consented to dispose of the sheep—if the farmer would give him a demijohn of peach brandy for his trouble.

Mike was a rip-roarer. "I can out-run, out-hop, out-jump, throw down, drag out, and lick any man in the country!" he used to say. "I am a Salt River roarer. I love the women, and I am chock-full of fight!" He wore "a bright red flannel shirt, covered by a loose blue coat . . . and coarse brown trousers of linsey-woolsey. His head-covering was a cap of untanned skin. . . ." He roamed the River for many years, and his memory ranged it after him.

For in 1822 Mike Fink's career came to an end. Leaving the River with a couple of companions named Carpenter and Tolbert he embarked on a trapping and hunting forage through the Missouri territory. Deep in the wilderness, Mike and Carpenter quarreled, but before they could come to

One of the Boldest Soldiers

blows Tolbert interceded. Mike, grudgingly, shook hands. The whiskey was uncorked.

In the old days along the River one of Mike's tricks with the rifle had been to shoot a tin cupful of whiskey off his companion's head. He proposed trying it now. Carpenter, resigned to his fate—"He knew he was going to be killed," said Tolbert—paced off the fifty yards; he balanced the whiskey cup on his cap. Mike Fink raised his rifle.

Mike Fink shot Carpenter clean through the middle of the forehead. Tolbert, as his friend fell, ran forward. "Is the whiskey spilt?" asked Mike calmly, swabbing out his rifle.

But that night—Mike had taken to the jug again: he was drunk and boasting—Tolbert shot him, killed him.

Rafts with a bark cabin for shelter, shanty-boats no bigger than skiffs drifted lazily from town to town: "Every trade is represented on these floating dens. Cobblers, tinsmiths . . . grocers, saloon-keepers, barbers. . . ." Like gypsies chaffering and bartering but stealing mostly, they floated along the landings, blowing their horns for customers.

Farmers in the middle valley, when the Fall crops were in, loaded their goods on home-made boats and set out down the Ohio, trading. For them the trip was a holiday: they cracked their heels and cut the pigeon-wing: "Even decent quiet deacons at home would throw aside religion and peace when they embarked on their annual trip down-river": they roared and stamped and rioted.

The great man-hunt for the Harpes through the eastern territory a few years earlier had driven thieves, cut-throats, rascals, prostitutes north and westward: they settled along the lower Ohio, where the river bends to join the Mississippi. From Red Bank to Fort Massac, the district had become a nest of piracy. The town of Red Bank itself, placed where the trace from Nashville joined the river, had become in a sense a headquarters for the outlaws. Now, as the traders, the farmers, the blustering boatmen rolled in, its viciousness increased.

No man is quite immune to his surroundings: in the early West the force of environment was almost physical in its intensity. In the wilderness, the slow monotonous days beat heavily against a man's will, but here in the river towns, in Red Bank, the attack was subtler. Fate was here all irony: one saw the honest man at his most gullible, the sharpster at his shrewdest; the drunken lout seemed ridiculous beside the cool-eyed gambler who robbed him; the traveler quaked piteously before the hard, determined bandit. Always the sinister suggestion, like the river at the bank, was sapping, prying: if it

One of the Boldest Soldiers

found the least flaw in a man's character it would enter and undermine all.

So in some measure it was with Samuel Mason. Coming west, he had settled at Red Bank. He had an honorable past, the record of a brave soldier in the Revolution; Van Cleve has told us that in its early efforts to establish order the Kentucky Legislature had commissioned him Justice of the Peace.

Yet in the end he weakened. He turned highwayman: doubtless, in his surroundings, it had come to seem a very brave thing to do. But in fact, thenceforward, he never made another brave move in his life; it was as if his whole nature crumbled.

He was all hypocrisy; he was always whining, pleading, protesting against "tyranny," against "persecution." Arrested, he turned welcher, double-crosser; brought to trial and shown the most complete proof of his guilt, he still almost hysterically proclaimed his innocence and in a certain mystical sense perhaps he believed it.

He had already been an old man when he turned bandit. He followed the Trace only five years before his capture and it was as if the sudden shifting in his character had left him swaying, dizzy: he leaned almost fearfully on his ancient manhood: he tried, as one might wrap a bundle with rotten twine, to tie up his present degradation with his former glory. His last quoted remark before he came to trial was a boast, pathetically incongruous: one night in the wilderness, having downed three pannikins of whiskey, he swore that "he was one of the boldest soldiers in the Revolutionary War, and there was no greater robber and no better niggerstealer than himself."

Hare was bold, hard, sure. The Harpes had their madness to hold them to their purpose. Mason, turning highwayman, turned craven: the fact, however, did not make him less dangerous to his victims.

Samuel Mason was born in Virginia in about the year 1750. He was twenty-five when Patrick Henry heard the clash of arms on the breeze that blew from the north and whipped the genteel Assembly into passionate patriotism. Mason caught the passion too. A burly strong young fellow, he joined the ranks of George Rogers Clark's "Long-Knives"; with them he floated down the Ohio, waded through swamps, startling French settlers and placating them again, pushing on across the wilderness of Illinois to the dramatic capture of the British General Hamilton at Vincennes. He withstood the hardship of the march, the danger of the attack with equal fortitude: his whole record through the Revolution was a brave one.

Later, settling after the War in the Kentucky territory, he bore himself well in the frontier defense:

once a party of twenty-eight men—himself among them—withstood for a day and night the attack of three hundred Indians: when the fight was over only Mason and one other survived.

We see him again in 1790—he is now aged forty, a solid substantial man; married, he has a son, a daughter and again two sons—he is dabbling in the chaotic government of the times: his name appears among those of other respectable citizens signing a petition to the General Assembly. A little later, by authority of the newly-constituted State, he is commissioned Justice of the Peace.

He is a tall man, grown heavier with his years but not fat, not ungainly: "He weighed about two hundred pounds, and was a fine-looking man." His face, however, holds one peculiarity: "a tooth which projected forwards, and could only be covered with his lip by an effort"; it makes him look a little wolfish but that does not matter; he is a good talker: a powerful pretentious persuasive man. One can picture him, portly pompous—but a little overweening in prosperity, swaggering a little in the light of his martial glory—pacing the town landing, parleying importantly with the merchants.

Yet even now the dark force of the wilderness is laboring at his passions. Solid and strict as the man might seem, somewhere within is the flaw, the weakness that sounds hollow against the striking of fate. And the crisis is coming.

"An infair was given to-day by Mason to a fellow named Kuykendall who had run away from Carolina on account of crimes and had run off with Mason's daughter to Diamond Island station a few weeks ago. The father had forbid him the house and threatened his life, but had become reconciled, and had sent for them to come home." Diamond Island was a blackleg haunt as evil-famed as the Cave-in-Rock. It would be a rankling thought for the vain J.P. that his daughter had chosen such companions. She was recalled, and her beau with her, perforce; Mason could even force a twisted smile at the story of their escapade:

"The parents and friends were highly diverted at the recital of the young couple's ingenuity in the courtship, and laughed heartily when the woman told of it. She said she had come downstairs after all the family had retired, having her petticoat around her, and returned with him through her parents' room, with the petticoat around both; and in the morning she brought him down in the same manner before daylight. . . ."

A stratagem that one would rather have expected to find related by a Brantôme than by a voyager among the rude and hearty pioneers but this is not the only time their own records gainsay the buttery recitals we have had of them. They were no better and no worse than ordinary men, but their feet were planted on the dark soil of the West and their souls fed on its profuse lustiness. Making textbook heroes of them we change them utterly, as the tangled wildflower is changed into the too perfect bud of the hothouse.

The beau bridegroom, however, seems to have been of a quite distinguished brutality: "This Kuykendall, I was told, always carried in his waistcoat pocket 'devil's claws'—instruments, or rather weapons, that he could slip his fingers in, and with which he could take off the whole side of a man's face at one claw!" Under any circumstances a dangerous man for a son-in-law and perhaps Samuel Mason had so concluded.

But the celebration went on. "We left them holding their frolic." One can picture it: the puncheon floor, the walls of chinked logs; split-bottom chairs, a table made of a halved log flat side uppermost; the fire roaring in the fireplace; the women with their linsey gowns and tightly coiled hair: the women with large hands, with faces pressed in the angular mold of labor; the men in buckskin breeches and tow-cloth shirt, stamping and guffawing.

It would be not quite night without, for their days ended early, but the gourd fiddle playing "Nappycot and petty-coat," "Billy in the wild woods"—the thin tunes would make the dusk seem deeper, the room warmer and brighter; there would be a jug of whiskey on the table.

There would be dancing: the "heel-and-toe," the "forward-and-back"; the couples vieing with each other as their spirits grew hot, whirling and stamping, cutting single and double pigeon-wings in the reel. "I think I see Boon Schoat bolting up to Sally Swarringame with:

" 'Now, Sal, you bantered me for a jig at t'other wedding, when you knowed I war too drunk to dance, but I'm your man now, and all right!'

" 'And I'm your gal,' replied Sally as she bounced to her feet. 'Jist wait till I git my shoes and stockings off. I never could dance worth a cent, with 'em on.'

"So, after tying a handkerchief around her waist and setting her comb down in her hair—while Boon was shucking his coat and girting himself—they went at it, and the way they made the puncheons rattle for half an hour was a terror to the rats beneath, cheered on by their friends. The men showed their gallantry by siding with Sally, while the women were equally magnanimous to Boon, and 'Hurraw, Boon!'—'Go to it, Sally!'—'Now you've got him!'—'Them's the licks!'—were alternately exclaimed during the set-to. . . ."

One can picture the flushed panting dancers whirl-

One of the Boldest Soldiers

ing and among them Samuel Mason, bouncing and bowing; one can see him tall portly pompous, filling and refilling the pannikins with whiskey. Kuykendall, swaying, grinning impudently, stands before him. Mason gives his daughter a pinch and she giggles; his lips squirm back from the fanged tooth and he smiles: he raises his cup in a toast to the wedding. Meanwhile, his two sons, and some of their companions, have slipped outside; are waiting in the darkness. Mason has made his plans.

And that night, outside in the underbrush, in the darkness, Kuykendall was killed. He was killed— by the sons, or by their companions: it is not known —because he interfered with Mason's ambitions. A stronger man would have killed the fellow himself. A more honorable man would have stayed behind, to answer for the act. But Mason's character had crumbled; the murder was for pride, but his pride would not sustain him: next day—his pretentions flung aside, his ambitions shattered—he was in full flight, his three sons with him. Among their companions was one Henry Havard, a young Tennesseean.

The flight was its own confession. Captain John Dunn—"the only recognized officer of the law in all this territory"—rode to intercept them. He was shot, his body left in a corn field.

Though Mason, as the most interested party, was

generally accused of this second murder, there was doubt enough to inculpate all. Young Havard was the first to appear in the settlements again: some months later, in company with a man named Samuel Mays and Mays' sister, a clubfoot girl, he rode into his father's homestead on the Red River in Tennessee. News of the murder had preceded him.

A party of Regulators—a citizen's posse—was immediately organized; their vengeance was swift and sure. They stormed the Havards' cabin. "They found Henry hid between two feather-beds"; they made short shrift of him. "They shot through the beds. They made the old man pull out the body of his son, and when they found his brains were oozing out they knew he was quite dead."

Mays and his lame sister, unregarded, escaped— Mays, ultimately, to play his rôle in Mason's final tragedy.

The Masons, meanwhile, had taken refuge at the Cave-in-Rock. They were not to remain there for long. It took long, in those days of dark voyagings, for suspicions to focus, for dangerous localities to become known. But at last, after so brutal a history of piracy, the Cave had been discovered as the nest of brigands it was. A fleet of flatboats, loaded with volunteers, was preparing at Pittsburgh to attack the stronghold.

One of the Boldest Soldiers

Hardly had Mason arrived before news of their danger reached the bandits. The gang split up. Mason—already his overbearing way, his preening manner had won him a certain prominence among the bandits—led a company of them to a new headquarters, to Wolf Island in the Mississippi, a few miles below the mouth of the Ohio. Here Audubon the naturalist, lazily voyaging down the River a year or two later, had wind of him and noted his zeal for organization: "He formed a line of worthless associates from the eastern part of Virginia to New Orleans." Mason's ambitions, now perverted, were driving him again.

A year later, in March, 1800, he appears in New Madrid, a river town opposite the Tennessee Line but in Spanish territory. He is well dressed, prosperous-looking; his manner "modest and unassuming . . . nothing of the raw-head-and-bloody-bones appearance which his character would indicate": he makes application for a passport. Like Thomas Hare before him, Mason has seen the advantage to be derived from the double frontier: a Spanish passport will permit him to slip back and forth from one jurisdiction to the other; its possession, moreover, generally passed current as a certificate of good character.

Certain formalities, however, must be met: for one, the recommendation of a citizen known to the

123

authorities must be had. Mason is ready for that. A too-trusting gentleman, met along the way and beguiled by the bandit's manner, deems it an honor to give the necessary assurances. The passport is granted. Mason slips quietly away; the town of New Madrid will not see him again for three years, but then in what changed circumstances!

In the Spring of the year 1801, Colonel Joshua Baker, a merchant and planter of Hardin County in Kentucky, embarked on his annual trading journey to New Orleans. The year had been good; crops were heavy: several flatboats were needed for the load of livestock and produce he was bringing to market.

It is not known when the party started; they lazied along down the River, enjoying the vacation: it was mid-summer before they reached New Orleans. Early in August, Colonel Baker set out on his return.

There were three men in the party, all mounted; they had with them also five pack-mules loaded with provisions and, rolled tight in buckskin bags and concealed among their supplies, the gold coin profits of the trip. Leaving Natchez a fourth man joined them, a Mr. Rogers, anxious of their company through the wilderness.

They rode slowly, being unhurried; the second morning, August 14, 1801, found them at Twelve-mile Creek, some ninety miles along the way. The Kentucky Gazette, in the issue for September 14, 1801, gives the account of what happened to them there. It is also the first newspaper notice of Mason's activities on the Trace.

"We are informed that on the fourteenth of August, about sixty miles on this side of the Big Biopiere River, Colonel Joshua Baker, a Mr. William Baker and a Mr. Rogers of Natchez, were robbed of their horses, travelling utensils, and about $2300 cash.

"It seems the company had halted in the morning at a small clear stream of water in order to wash. As soon as they had dismounted and gone to the water four men appeared, blacked, between them and their horses and demanded surrender of their money and property, which they were obliged to comply with.

"Mr. W. Baker was more fortunate than his companions. A pack-horse, on which was a considerable sum of money, being frightened at the appearance of the robbers, ran away, and they being in haste to escape could not pursue. Mr. W. Baker recovered his horse and money. He, however, lost his riding-horse, etc.

"Colonel Baker and Mr. Rogers came to the first settlement, where they procured assistance and immediately went in pursuit of the villains. It is to be hoped they will be apprehended.

"One of them who was described by Colonel Baker, formerly resided at Red Banks. A brother of Colonel Baker, our informant, obtained this information from Mr. W. Baker, who lodged at his house in Lexington on Thursday night last."

And so a new terror usurped the dark wilderness. The Harpes had gone—one slaughtered, beheaded; the other vanished—but scarcely had men's fears been lightened of their menace before this other took its place.

And again men moved warily, passed wide; joined forces for company and then scanned the other's face closely, dreading treachery. "Frequently men would wait at the line to come through with the mail carrier. John B. Craighead, of Nashville, was once employed to take some boats with produce down the river to Natchez, which he sold at that place.

"On his return home, he stopped at the line of the Indian country so as to come through with Mr. Swaney, who was carrying the mail. They started just at nightfall. The night was cloudy, but the moon shone out occasionally. . . ."

One can picture it, that long-gone evening: the

tall trees, their roots moss-coated, their branches shaggily spreading high over the two men's heads; the acres of desolation, grown thick with cane the cage of silence, and crackling as if the very silence strained in the net; the whole alternately clouded and split with pale light again fantastically, as the sky cleared and changed; and the two men, riding silently.

"They had gone eight or ten miles when they discovered two men on horseback and carrying guns in their rear." They had felt a menace, flitting and intangible, all about them; now in those two stalking figures behind them it had materialized at last.

They rode on. There was nothing else to do. Craighead was in a panic. Swaney sent him ahead with the pack-animals; he rode behind in the narrow path. The two dark strangers followed relentlessly. "The robbers would frequently come up to within two hundred yards of them, but never spoke. In this way they trailed them for about two hours." It was apparent that the bandits, sure of their power, were waiting the most favorable moment to strike. And Swaney remembered that just ahead of them, the Trace twisted through a thick clump of cane, a jungle of underbrush. He told Craighead. He told him "he dreaded to pass through this place"; they would be helpless there.

The two men rode on, debating. Should they make

a stand? Should they run for it? And suddenly, in the midst of their deliberation—it was as if nature itself had relented, as if all fate had made a single dizzying turn—they saw a pin-prick of light! "They saw a light some distance off the road, and went to it.

"They found some Indians encamped, and Mr. Swaney got two of them to slip down in the direction of the road and ascertain what had become of the two men who had followed them.

"In a few minutes the Indians returned and reported that the two men had dismounted and were taking positions behind trees." Swaney knew the bandits would wait till day if need be: daylight and night time were equal in the wilderness.

"Mr. Swaney told Craighead that then was the time to elude their pursuers, and mounting their horses, they struck out through the woods and kept parallel with the road for about three quarters of a mile, when they returned to the road; then, quickening their pace to a gallop, they rode on ten or twelve miles without stopping, leaving the robbers far behind." Craighead was liberal with the spur: he had a deadly fear to speed him: "Mr. Craighead would not consent to stop to feed their tired horses or to eat anything themselves until nearly noon next day. . . ."

Swaney, riding almost weekly through the Trace, had many a brush with the bandits. Passing, Mason himself would often halt the mail carrier: "He was always anxious to know what was said of him by the public." He would ask news of the towns, of events; the bandit and the rider would chat peacefully a bit, by the roadway; even in these short interviews the strange hypocrisy of the man, his frantic clutching at respectability is evident: he hints at oppression and betrayal; his lip skims back from the wolf-tooth and he swears that he has been driven to the wilderness, that he abhors bloodshed; all he asks is justice.

But if he seeks justice he goes about it deviously. There was another night:

"That night Mr. Swaney was very sleepy, and stopped after dark, made his horse fast, wrapped himself in his blanket and slept soundly until about a hour before daybreak, and found that he had slept longer than he should. Mounting his horse he started at a lively gait, and just at daylight he was descending a little hill to the Boage Tuckalo. . . ." One can see him topping the rise in the dew of the morning with the tree tops, emerald-green in the sunlight, beneath him. He heard voices, somewhere concealed below.

"He heard some loud talking. Hoping it was the boatmen, who were always anxious to give Mr. Swaney something to eat and in return to get from him the news, he began to blow on his bugle and rushed down the hill." He stumbled on the climax of swift tragedy.

He heard a man's voice shout, "Surrender!" He heard a shot, and another shot. A great tree had obscured his view but as he passed it he saw a mounted traveler, pale, cursing helplessly, his emptied pistols smoking in his hands; facing him, a bandit, his features unrecognizable in war-paint, his musket raised.

Coolly, the robber fired. The man on horseback jerked about suddenly, then fell face forward, his body slipping down across the saddle-horn. "He fell across the path with his pistols in his hands." At the shot, Swaney's horse had shied; his hoofs caught in the underbrush and the letter carrier, clinging, was almost thrown. In that instant the robber vanished, darting swiftly into the canebrake. When Swaney had his mount under control (it took but a moment) the Trace lay clear and sunny again, save for the one, the traveler, who lay sprawling, dead.

Across the hollow Swaney heard the sound of galloping horses pounding up the hill. Putting spurs to his own mount, he soon overtook two men, terrified, riding furiously back along the trail: the one—a Major Ellis—was a friend, and the other the young son of the slain man. His name had been Robert McAlpin; his home was on the Apalachie River, in Georgia.

Guided by the letter carrier, they rode on to an

One of the Boldest Soldiers

Indian settlement known as the Pigeon Roost, to get reënforcements. A few of the Indians agreed to help them, and so the little cavalcade rode back again to the scene of the murder. When they returned, they found that the robbers had been there in the meantime. McAlpin's horse had been taken, and with it all the money in his saddlebags; the body had been stripped to the underwear. Curiously, however, a belt of money which he had worn around his waist next the skin, had not been noticed. Young McAlpin—he was a boy in his teens—took the belt and tied it in his saddle roll.

There was not much they could do. Swaney and Ellis cast about, here and there, in the canebrake, seeking trace of the bandits' trail. They found none. The Indians were in a hurry to be off. So at last, with some cut branches, they roughed away the soil in a shallow hole, laid in the body, and covered it well with stones. Before leaving—the boy had watched everything, white-faced, silent—"Young McAlpin . . . cut a large chip from a tree, made the place smooth, and cut on it with his pocket-knife:

" 'ROBT. McALPIN
MURDERED & KILLED
HERE JULY 31' "

Mason had now been something more than a year on the Trace, and yet it is doubtful if at this time the man considered himself definitely committed to a career of outlawry. In those days the conception of law was crude, Germanic: a man was judged on his own cognizance, and his past was rarely inquired into. So often, when an affair of love or of credit grew too pressing or when a brawl had ended bloodily, a man would disappear from the settlements: he would wander, hunting with the Indians, living —all life was predatory then—in any way he could; years later, perhaps, he would reappear stepping silently out of the wilderness, to resume his customary existence.

Thus Jim Allen, at the Chickasaw Agency. Thus Sam Houston—a young lawyer, in eight years' practice he had risen to be elected Governor of Tennessee; he was respected, handsome, "of gallant bearing, standing six foot six in his socks, and his fine features were lit up by large, eagle-looking eyes" —suddenly, one day, his friend Willoughby Williams found him sitting in a room at the Nashville Inn: "I am a ruined man. I will exile myself," he was saying. No one knew what had happened, but his wife had broken with him; he had resigned his office. That night, in disguise, he left town, traveling north, eating "a little common hog and hominy and sleeping on his own blanket before the fire" at wayside inns. He joined the Cherokees, in the tribe of the noted Chief Jolly: once he marched with them, unrecognized in the feathers and paint of a Cherokee warrior, through the very streets of Nashville. He came back to the towns three years later; before he died he had commanded the Federal troops in the war with Mexico, and had been twice elected President, and once Governor, of Texas.

There were many similar metamorphoses among less famous personages; perhaps Mason, lurking in the wilderness with his sons, and his son's wife, and her two children, still hoped to be a Justice of the Peace again.

The killing of Kuykendall at Red Bank had been of a nature that was readily excusable in that time. The murder of Captain Dunn was another matter but Havard had paid for that; besides, the Kentucky settlements were far away. As for his activities along the Trace, there were few victims who had survived to identify him, and these few were scattered all over the river country. A man must trust to luck. And he was one who hankered after respectability; he was fat with his own self-esteem.

So he hung about the Trace when the letter carrier was passing; he quizzed him about the towns and the politics and the people; with his mildest face he protested that he only asked for justice, and a chance to reëstablish himself among honest men. And at last, one day in the Fall of 1801, he and his son John rode down to Natchez, to put the matter to the proof.

THE END OF MASON

NATCHEZ, at the beginning of the century, was already rising toward the commanding position it was soon to occupy and for fifty years to maintain on the lower River: in commerce, second only to New Orleans; in beauty, "the handsomest city in America, next to Charlestown"; in romance, richest of them all.

Everywhere about it lay the virgin wilderness, but here—and from here southward through the Spanish country—how extravagant and various in growth!

Trees: "the black-willow, the black-ash, water maple, pecan, pawpaw, cypress, sweet-bay, magnolia, katalpa, persimmon, locust, dogwood, wild plum, tulip-tree, white-oak, black-oak, swamp-oak, chestnut-oak, the red cedar, broom pine, buck-eye, wild cherry, palmetto or 'cabbage tree,' cassina yapon (from which the Creeks and other Indian tribes make their 'black drink' liquor for councils and festivals), the beech, the chestnut, the chincopin. . . ."

Many of these, in their abundant foliage and wealth of bloom, might almost seem more flower than tree but twining among them, palely or gaudily

"The city of Natchez occupies a very handsome situation. It is built on a hill nearly perpendicular, of about two hundred feet in height from the surface of the River. This hill is called the Bluff. The city contains about three hundred houses."

—*An engraving from "Das Illustrierte Mississippithal."*

"From the mouth of the Arkansas River, on the west bank of the Mississippi, there is no settlement until you come to the town of New Madrid."
—An engraving by Henry Lewis from "Das Illustrierte Mississippithal."

The End of Mason

petaled, "the China root, the passion flower, mimosa instia, saracinia, three or four handsome species of the water-dock, poke, sumac several species; many vines, as the trumpet flower, the mistletoe. . . ."

Through all this, forever winding, forever rolling, the mighty River: "Its margins are not wanting in musick, from a great variety of 'sweet songsters of the wood' "; the pelican—"It is asserted that they are very fond of musick; their pouches are frequently dried and converted into bags and purses, for the use of the ladies"—had its haunt along the River. "The banks of the River, especially below Natchez, are lined with groves of Orange trees, whose delightful fragrance and the beautiful appearance of their flowers, has a charming effect on the feelings. Here the *bois d'arc* (bow-wood) or yellow dyewood, is sometimes seen. It bears a gold-colored fruit as large as the egg of the ostrich; its deep green foliage resembles that of the Orange tree; and no forest tree can compare with it for ornamental grandeur. . . ."

In the midst of this luxuriance, where the Trace and the Spanish Road and the few straggling plantation trails fed in like a tangle of wilderness vines and knotted at the city's center, stood Natchez.

"The city of Natchez occupies a very handsome situation. It is built on a hill nearly perpendicular of about 200 feet in height above the surface of the River." Below, on a narrow clay shelf between the base of the Bluff and the River, lay the Landing: in Murrel's time this spot would be famous all over the country as "Natchez-under-the-Hill . . . the nucleus of vice upon the Mississippi"; already it was "covered with a number of dwellings, low taverns, dram-shops and trading houses" for the flatboat-men whose craft lay moored in ranks along the shore.

"At the foot of the bluffs are long straggling lines of wooden buildings. Above, a pile of gray and white cliffs with here and there a church steeple, a roof elevated above its summit, and a lighthouse hanging on the verge. The whole appearance of the place is highly romantic." Thus from the River; it was not until one climbed the steep path up the hill, lined with "Orange and Liquor shops," that he entered the true city, Natchez itself.

Natchez: the town was booming. Doctor Nutt, bringing cotton seed from Mexico, had planted it at the settlement of Petit Gouffre—Petty Gulf, later, Rodney—thirty miles upriver from Natchez and now all over the lower country the land was being cleared and fields laid in seed: "Many of the cotton plantations yield from $5,000 to $20,000 a year. The owners indulge in every luxury, and set an example in dissipation." Natchez catered to them. "The vice of Natchez is proverbial throughout America."

The End of Mason

Natchez: "It contains about 300 houses, and 2500 inhabitants." There was a pulse in the place, as two temperaments—Spanish and American—met, jangled, or joined in a curious throbbing overtone. "The houses in Natchez are mostly frame, with a great many doors and windows, for the admission of the cool breezes, in the hot months; they are low, being generally but one story high": they were, for the most part, Spanish-built; so was the theater, "a large commodious building, constructed of brick, with arched entrances." The iron grill-work and vaulted corridors within the principal buildings reflected the same foreign architecture; without, the shallow-sloping roofs, extending far beyond the walls to shelter the tiered piazzas or galleries and supported by arcades of slender columns, marked how the Spanish style had changed and altered.

Natchez: "The principal street runs east from the edge of the bluff." Here were the banks, the fancy-stores—they were rather like bazaars: "The stores are turned inside out every morning, to adorn their fronts and create zig-zags on the sidewalks," while among the piles of merchandise strewn all over the walk, the pedestrian must pick his way as best he might. But few men walked. "A circumstance that soon arrests the attention of the stranger is the number of gentlemen with riding whips in their hands. Here all are horsemen." Ladies drove in from their plantations in gigs, and were wheeled through the esplanade at the edge of the Bluff in well-appointed carriages but even then the husband or lover who attended them rode usually on his own mount, beside the carriage wheel. Most of the men wore "white blanket coats and broad-brimmed white hats; this is the dress of the planters."

Wealth was profuse, almost unavoidable among the landed classes, but life still held a frontier aspect: on the plantations, many a costly dining-table set with silver teetered on a home-made puncheon floor; in Natchez, men strolled and drawled, fought duels, chaffered·for slaves, drank themselves under the table, were cheated by commission merchants and gambled wildly on their own horses at the races— all in a curious mixture of the uncouth and the elegant that is difficult for us to picture to-day.

Women were held in almost Turkish seclusion, save when one of the great public balls enlivened the season; then they went attired in lace and jewels, surrounded by a rosy haze of chivalry. Men, marrying late, retained all their lives the pleasantest attributes of bachelorhood: they lounged about the bars, occupied the life of the town, haunted the slave sales, dined in groups of cronies at the inns.

Natchez: its strange punctilio, its unexpected barbarisms; its dreaming mansions, jessamine-shaded, and its raucous, teeming streets: "negroes, negresses,

The End of Mason

fashionably-dressed young men with slender riding-whips in their hands, wild fellows in linsey-woolsey, with long locks hanging over their eyes and shoulders, Kentucky boatmen"—into all this, riding suddenly out of the wilderness, came Mason.

He had a friend in Natchez: Anthony Glass (or Gass) was his name. This Glass, in the town, had the reputation of an honest merchant; he had his store, well-stocked in dry-goods, hardware and general merchandise; he was prosperous, affable, a good mixer: in reality, for Mason, he filled the double rôle of "fence" and informer, sending word ahead to the bandit when a rich prize was coming up the Trace, or warehousing and marketing a boat-load of produce, when Mason robbed along the River.

So now, when the robber wanted to mingle with the quality, his agent helped him out. He saw to his rooms at Walton's tavern; he towed the fat-faced, heavy-bodied interloper about the town, introducing him vaguely as a planter from upstate, hinting still more cautiously that his protegé had a pocket of gold for spending.

And for a time their little deception prospered, until one day—perhaps as he lounged at the Market, slapping his riding-crop against his waxed boots; perhaps as, with his long head tilted sidewise, he sipped his glass at Monsieur Ude's and raised his

139

whining voice in the tap-room conversation—one day Mason was recognized.

One can picture it: the loitering group suddenly disrupted; the stranger pointing, accusing; Mason staring, mouth agape: "That's the man! The man that robbed Baker!" For the town, it was a seven days' sensation. For Mason, it was the collapse of all his hopes.

With his son, he was thrust in the old stone-walled Spanish jail. Together, a few days later, they appeared for trial. The Baker robbery appears to have been the only charge brought against them, and a clever pleader—Wallace, by name—did his best to mitigate their share in that: he won the sympathy of some of the populace, but not of the magistrates. The sentence handed down was: thirty-nine lashes each, publicly administered, and followed by twelve hours in the town pillory.[1]

The town turned out to watch the spectacle, and to learn how men, by sheer insisting, can almost make their own lies true. For Mason, through it all, still

[1] This was mild punishment. There were at that time no less than eleven crimes which carried the penalty of death, ranging from murder, arson, rape, through forgery, manslaughter or horse stealing (second offense) to slave stealing and selling a free person for a slave: an inclusive list. The penalty for a first conviction of horse stealing in Tennessee was that the offender be "branded with a red-hot iron on the right cheek with the letter H, and on the left with the letter T, stand in the pillory one hour, be publicly whipped on his bare back with 39 lashes well laid on, and at the same time have both his or her ears nailed to the pillory and cut off." It was not until about 1829, when the Penitentiary system was generally adopted in the West, that these ferocious penalties were appreciably modified. Mason, therefore, it will be seen, got off easy.

clung to his martyr's rôle. As the whip fell, and they hung there, backs bared, sweating and straining with the pain of it, their cry was, "Innocent!" still. "I witnessed the flogging, and I shall never forget their cries of 'Innocent!' at every blow of the cowhide. Until the last lash was given, they shrieked with the same despairing cry of 'Innocent! Innocent!'"

Whipped, they were locked neck and wrist in the pillory; to Mason, this was the bitterest punishment of all. No one can tell what savage thoughts he had, clamped in the uncouth device while the townsmen gawked, but by his future actions they must have been savage indeed. Released, he celebrated his freedom by the first act of wild and abandoned defiance that this schemer—so smooth and calculating before —had ever been known to commit: "The elder Mason and his son, they shaved their heads, and stripping themselves naked, mounted their horses and yelling like Indians, rode through and out of the town." So, roaring drunk, obscene and turbulent, the two kicked along the dusty streets of Natchez and vanished.

A few days later, one of the jurors at the trial rode out toward the Trace. He was stopped just beyond the town limits: Mason, lurking there, leaped out and confronted him. The fellow flopped from his horse, pleading and crying: he had a wife, children; they would starve. "I've got a wife," said Mason.

"Children, too." He raised his gun. "Did I ever do you any harm?" he demanded. No, said the other. "Did you ever hear of me murdering anybody?" No, said the other. In the end, Mason kicked him over, spat in his face: "You ain't worth killing!" he said, and rode away.

That was the last to be seen of Mason for a long time. But the killings, the robberies went on. Mr. Anthony Glass, now a little suspect among the merchants of Natchez, rode north along the Trace; with him, all unsuspecting, traveled a rich Kentuckian, Campbell by name. Campbell's body was found later, robbed and mutilated, in the cane; crudely marked on a nearby tree was a legend: "Done By Mason Of The Woods." Glass, a month or two afterward, turned up in the town of Walnut Hills and started in business all over again.

A party of Kentucky boatmen, roaming up the Trace, had camped "in what was called Gum Springs, in the Choctaw Nation." They were making ready for the night when one man, rummaging in the underbrush, stepped full on a robber lying there. The bandit fired his gun, yelled for the attack; in an instant the camp was in a turmoil, the Kentuckians, half-clothed, leaping panic-stricken away among the trees.

The End of Mason

They stayed there, quaking and starting, all night through. In the morning, the letter carrier came up with them. "Mr. Swaney came along, and seeing the campfires burning, rode about, but could find no one. He knew something was wrong, and began to blow his bugle." One by one, the boatmen appeared, crawling miserably out of their hiding-places. "They were the worst scared, worst looking set of men he ever saw, some of them having but little clothing on, and one big fellow had only a shirt.

"They immediately held a sort of council of war"; they decided to make a fight of it. Everything had been taken, their firearms as well as their money, but that did not discourage them. Each man seized a knotted branch, a heavy stone, and they set off together, whooping and swearing and loudly boasting: they would rush on the robbers, belt them and flay them; they would meet their fire and withstand it, and if a few fell in the first volley, let the remainder rush in with their shillalehs, to revenge their comrades.

Leading them all, ran the shirt-tailed giant, implacable—until he found his pants. "The big Kentuckian found his pants, in the waistband of which he had sewed four doubloons and, to his great joy, the robbers had not found them. After this it was noticed that the big Kentuckian's valor began to fail him, and he was soon in the rear." The rest plowed

on through the cane, finding here and there dis-
carded fragments of their property—saddle-bags,
trousers, jackets—ripped and plundered. Their fury
was fading; those in the lead found excuses to linger,
those in the rear nudged them on.

So they came to where the robbers waited for
them. "They were suddenly hailed by Mason and
his men, who were hid behind trees, with their guns
presented." At this the lurching little mob halted,
gulped—"Clear out!" yelled the bandits. "We'll kill
every last one of ye!"—and stampeded. "The big
Kentuckian outdistanced the whole party in the race
back to camp."

The tale of Mason and the big Kentuckian's pants
was to be told again and again, and greeted with
shouts of laughter, around many a frontier fireside,
but most of the bandit's escapades had a grimmer
cast. He had developed a wild new audacity, a kind
of blatant vengefulness. He placarded his crimes; he
scrawled "Mason" in the blood of his victims.

He was seldom seen; never again did Swaney
meet him, unctuous and plausible, waiting along the
Trace. Once, after a peculiarly bitter massacre, a
party of men set out in search of him. He had become elusive, a flitting menace; no one knew his
hiding-place but by good luck, finally, they sighted
him and the chase went crashing through the cane.

The End of Mason

But Mason outdistanced them; they lost the trail, found it again; in the late afternoon they came down to the edge of a lonely bayou where the robber must have passed. As they hesitated there, choosing a crossing, a rifle spoke from the opposite thicket; one of their men fell, killed. Across the water, a figure appeared, waving his arms wildly. "Do ye want Mason? I'm Mason!" he yelled, and plunged away.

It was obvious that his organization was growing. His men robbed the River and the Trace simultaneously. On February 10, 1802, the new Governor of the Mississippi Territory, William C. C. Claiborne, wrote to the Spanish Governor General of the Province of Louisiana; he stated that a number of daring robberies had been committed "upon some citizens of the United States who were descending the River Mississippi on their passage to this town (Natchez)." He pointed out that it was "uncertain whether the bandits were Spanish or American," and he hinted, in the cautious diplomatic way, that he would be glad to concur in any system of policing the common frontier which would help in capturing the outlaws.

On February 28, the Spanish Governor General Manuel de Salcedo replied. He was a little querulous. He pointed out that he had given his officers "the most positive orders to take the most efficacious means of discovering and apprehending the criminals that can be adopted, and I assure your Excellency that if the criminals are taken they will be punished in such manner as to serve as an example to others." He took occasion to complain, however, that the "people of the States and Western Settlements, having the freedom and use of the navigation of the Mississippi," came down into the Spanish province in great numbers, among them many "vagabonds who have fled from, or who do not, or cannot return to, the United States."

Claiborne had been working toward some reciprocal agreement by which the police of either commonwealth might be permitted to pursue criminals across the boundary into the jurisdiction of the other. But the Spanish Governor General had his own ax to grind, and the suggestion was disregarded.

A month or two after this exchange of notes had been made, Colonel Baker appeared again in Natchez. He had again run foul of Mason and his men, this time on the River, flatboating his produce down to New Orleans. He reported the incident directly to Governor Claiborne: how a troop of bandits in pirogues, led by Mason, had boarded him; how a battle had followed, and how, eventually, the robbers had been driven off, but not before several men on either side had been wounded.

The Governor took action, sending letters to all commanders of military outposts along the River or the Trace, informing them that Baker, as well as many others, had been attacked, "near the mouth of the Yazou River," and urging them to search out the robbers and capture them. The letters contained one detail of gruesome importance: it was related that "a certain Wiley Harpe" was believed to be a member of Mason's gang.

And so again, like some pale flower of vicious odor and uncertain season, the memory of the terrible Harpes bloomed along the wilderness trails. For five years the elder brother's head had moldered in the crotched tree near Red Bank and men had almost forgotten that Little Harpe, with the "downcast countenance," was still at large.

Men had hoped, if they considered the matter at all, that he had left the country, that he had died, that in some obscure affray of knives or pistols he had been killed; learning that he lived, a kind of superstitious terror engulfed them. Men went about wondering, muttering: where in those three dark years had he been wandering?—what mad deeds had his fury driven him to?—what strange events and unrecorded disappearances, until then unexplained and half forgotten, had marked his bloody passage?

147

The Outlaw Years

Later, digging as among gnarled roots in the twisted testimony at Mason's trial, they were to unearth the answers to a few of the questions. There was the tale of young Bass, a Tennessee farmer: riding north along the Trace, a stranger had accosted him. They rode along together; Bass was not well: he had a "misery" in his stomach; the stranger was most helpful along the way. So they rode on to the Bass homestead; there the stranger lingered a few days, to rest. When he rode away again, young Bass' sister rode with him: he had courted her, married her; they were setting out for North Carolina together.

A few days later, the stranger returned to the settlement, alone. With looks full of sorrow, he related how his young wife's horse had run away; she had been thrown, dragged; before he could help her, she was dead. People believed him; there was no reason to do otherwise: in the end he had sold her few belongings and ridden away again. Later, when by chance they suspected that Harpe and the amiable stranger were identical, they opened the grave: the girl had been beaten to death, and cruelly mutilated afterward.

But as for now, all this was still mystery and vague conjecture—a kind of fog of doubt and foreboding, in which men saw Mason and his still more terrible partner Little Harpe moving, evilly peering. A few

The End of Mason

weeks after Claiborne's communication, rewards totaling $2000 had been offered for their capture.

A month later, definite news was had that the gang's hideout lay near the Rocky Springs, forty miles north of Natchez along the Trace. A general hunt was started. Men plunged into the thicket, reached the camp, but found it deserted. Thwarted, they spent their energies digging for the treasure the bandits were supposed to have buried there. They found none; none has ever been found but there are still vague rumors that Mason's hoard lies somewhere there, sunk in the swampy ground.

While the posses dug for gold, the letter carrier met the young wife of Tom Mason, stumbling along the Trace. "When Mr. Swaney met her she was making her way through the Chickasaw Nation on foot carrying her baby." The rest had abandoned her, pregnant: she had borne the child, alone, in the wilderness. "Mrs. Mason begged Mr. Swaney to assist her, allowing her to ride until he got tired walking, when she would walk and let him ride and hold the child." So he brought her down to Natchez; she revealed that the others had fled across the River, into Spanish territory. Soon after, the rumor passed that the robbers had set up headquarters on Stack Island, also called "Crow's Nest," in the Mississippi about fifty miles north of Vicksburg.

The Outlaw Years

The robberies, murders, continued. The Frankfort, Kentucky, Palladium quoted "a letter, dated Natchez, June 11, from a gentleman who lately descended the River, containing the following intelligence: 'We were attacked by robbers near the mouth of the White River. They hailed us from the shore, telling us they wished to purchase rifles, and on our refusing to land, they commenced the pursuit, in pirogues, having in each six men well armed. They were commanded by a person named Mason, who scours the road through the wilderness.' "

This was a common stratagem of Mason's. A merchant named Owsley, lazying down the River, had been hailed from shore by a party of men. They were emigrants, they said; they needed rifles and would pay well for them. When the bargain had been made, the loaded guns were suddenly presented at Owsley's head; he and his crew were put in the small-boat and set adrift. He was lucky to escape with the loss of his stores; another boatload of travelers, held up at the point of their own weapons, were killed to a man, their bodies disembowelled and sunk, their goods sent on down to Vicksburg and sold to Anthony Glass. "He will never betray us," said Mason.

No one betrayed him. With a price on his head, with the police of two nations scouring both sides of the River in his search, with all travelers warned of his exploits and his name known all through the wil-

The End of Mason

derness, he yet survived for six months longer. In the end, he betrayed himself.

On January 11, 1803, one Pierre Dapron, shuffling and embarrassed, appeared before the Spanish magistrates in the town of New Madrid. Asked his business, he related that he had just returned from the settlement of Little Prairie, some twenty miles downstream; while there, his friend Ignace Belan, a *voyageur,* had told him of having seen four men loitering at the outskirts of the town; Belan believed them to be members of the Mason gang, and had asked him to report the matter.

The magistrates looked wise, and considered the information; in the end, they decided to instigate a quiet inquiry among such citizens of Little Prairie as might have come to Court Day. Almost immediately, they uncovered fresh news.

Georges Ruddell, among others, admitted that he had seen the newcomers. According to him, there were eight men and one woman in the party. They had arrived a week before, well armed and well mounted. They had rented ten acres and a house from a farmer named Lesieur; they seemed peaceable and industrious. There was but one thing about them that was suspicious: one man, heavily armed, was always posted like a sentinel at the cabin door; they seemed wary of passers-by. The magistrates deemed it advisable to turn the matter over to the police, for investigation.

Next day a party of four men, headed by "Don Robert McCoy, Captain of the Militia," rode down to Little Prairie. A dozen regulars under Corporal Felipo Canot had already been detailed there, to assist him. Hardly had the little party dismounted, jingling their spurs, in the village green, before Mason himself appeared.

All honest-eyed and unctuous, he greeted the astonished commander. He asked news of New Madrid, if the court still held. "I hear there's talk going around, about me," he said. "I'm a decent man, and I'm sick of these stinking tales. I hear only a couple of days ago somebody was up before the Court spreading false accusations against me. I'm going up there myself and set matters square. I want to live in peace."

McCoy was no fool. He decided to play up to the man's story. "I suppose you've got your passports?" he demanded. "Yes," Mason told him. "Well," said McCoy, "I'm just down here on inspection tour and it's no affair of mine, but I did hear that there was a complaint about you. Now, I've got some business to attend to about town first, but if you want to, after that, you can get your people together and I'll come over to your cabin and check up your papers. Then I can report back to the Commandant to-night and if

The End of Mason

·erything's all right you won't have to go to town
all." Mason, gratefully, agreed; it was a good idea.
That afternoon, when McCoy, alone save for an
:derly, rode up to the cabin, the whole family
waited him. The Captain bustled about, opened his
ossier, settled himself at a table. Then he looked
pout the room where all had been gathered. "Is
verybody here?" he demanded. Mason beamed.
Yes indeed, your Excellency," he chanted.

"Then arrest them!" shouted McCoy. Mason,
/hitefaced, started to his feet but he was too late.
'he house had been surrounded; the militiamen
oured in, guns ready. "Do you call this fair treat-
ient?" Mason demanded, almost weeping. McCoy
:dered them all to be put in chains.

They gave their names: Samuel Mason and his
·ns, Thomas, John, Samuel Junior; John Taylor;
larguerite Douglas, wife of John Mason, and her
ree children. Then, in the laborious Spanish way,
ι inventory of their belongings was taken: it in-
uded a hoard of bolted silk, muslin and cotton,
,000 in United States money and a miscellany of
ld and silver pieces, numerous rifles and pistols old
id new, a field stove, camp equipment—even such
ivial items as a box of salt and a side of bacon were
ted. This done, they were transported to New Ma-
:id. On the morning of January 17 they were
·ought to trial.

The Outlaw Years

The trial itself is a curious record of pompo[us]
jurisprudence and frontier offhandedness. The Cou[rt]
was Spanish, but testimony was taken in Frencl[;]
it was then read, translated, to the deponents, wh[o]
signed it. No attempt at cross-examination appea[rs]
to have been made, save in the occasional interje[c]
tions of the examining magistrates: each witness—
and they were innumerable: townsmen, traveler[s,]
tavern-keepers—was called, sworn "on the cro[ss]
of his sword ·and by the Holy Scriptures" [to]
tell the truth, and then each was allowed to tell h[is]
story. The magistrates were soon adrift in a welte[r]
ing sea of fact, conjecture and miscellaneous hypotl[l]
eses but occasionally, as lie follows lie eddyin[g]
around the circle, we see the figures of Mason an[d]
Taylor, like two men caught in a whirlpool [of]
strange passionate hatred, spinning, staring, sinkin[g.]

Mason's turn came first: he broke out immediate[ly]
into a sorrowful tale of persecution. Other men[’s]
crimes had hounded him all through the wildernes[s:]
he had been driven out of Natchez, he had bee[n]
driven from the River, he had been driven acro[ss]
the border—he had enemies unprecedented in the[ir]
maliciousness—by a tyranny of false accusation. An[d]
now, an old man, broken, coming to settle on Spani[sh]
soil and start life over again, he was met at the ve[ry]
outset by an echo of the same pernicious conspirac[y.]
He was an honest man. It was a little hard.

The End of Mason

Where had he gotten the money, the seven thou-
and dollars? He had found it in a bag, hanging on
bush near the site where one night, in the wilder-
ess, they had camped. Travelers, fearing such rob-
ers as he had libellously been nominated, often hid
heir cash in the thicket: this, he supposed, had been
orgotten by some careless traveler; he was only
eeping it in trust, for the rightful claimant.

Why had he lived hidden, never appearing to an-
wer his charges? He knew how strong a case his
iemies had made against him. Why was he known
) have consorted with ruffians and criminals? Be-
iuse honest people had cruelly spurned him. But
ow, though it cost him his life—but was it not the
istom to ease the sentence of a man who offered
nportant information to the State?—he would tell
l. The Commandant admitted that such information
'as construed as a sign of repentance and was usu-
lly met with lenient treatment. Mason whispered
iat John Taylor—"And he sometimes goes by other
imes which I can not recall"—was one of the guilty.

Mason, blown with a kind of puffing self-right-
usness, stepped down. Taylor testified. Unlike the
indy Mason, he spoke little and answered sullenly:
He was always downcast and fierce, his hair red,
s face meager and his stature below that of the
'erage man." But he grew eager in his own vindi-

155

cation; he grafted his own lies neatly enough
those of Mason.

True enough, his name was not Taylor; it w
Setton—John Setton. He was an Irishman born; ha
come to America in 1797 and enrolled as a soldi
but he had soon deserted "near the high coast":
was then he had changed his name. Thereafter, l
had wandered out through the wilderness. He w
an honest man and a workingman: once at Nogal
across from Vicksburg he had worked three wee
"for His Majesty the King of Spain," after which
had signed as carpenter aboard the "row-gall
Louisiana" and worked his way down-river to No
Orleans. He had lived anyhow, as a man might, b
always honestly. For two years, he had "hunted wi
the Chaquetaw Indians," but that had ended whe
in Arkansaw territory, he was recognized by a form
officer of his and jailed as a deserter.

It was thus he had been led to the Masons. With
man named Wiguens, another soldier, he had a
caped from jail; Wiguens, an evil fellow, had intr
duced him to Samuel Mason.

Here the Commandant halted him: "You say yo
name is Setton?"—"Setton, sir."—"Do you know t
name, or the man, Harpe?"

There was a moment of silence, a heavy silent m
ment while Setton gulped, hesitated. He did n

know the man, he said at last, but he had "heard of the name." He went on with his story.

His life with the Masons had been the history of one long fruitless attempt to escape. A dozen times he had tried to run away, always to be caught, recaptured. Once at a settlement, when a "military gentleman" had been pointed out to him as the leader of a search-party, he had edged near the man, had tried to attract his attention: Mason had come up behind him with the point of a dagger pricking his side. They took him away, and kept him bound and gagged for days. From that time on, he had been allowed neither powder nor firearms: to escape then, in the wilderness, would have been suicide.

And again, threatening death, they had made him sign all manner of false affidavits, confessing the Owsley robbery, confessing the robbery of Campbell and Glass—"though it was known that Glass was Mason's man at Natchez"—confessing that he had robbed Baker on the Trace, and had taken "twenty-five hundred piasters in gold, silver and bank-notes."

So he went on, lumping all the random accusations he could think of, against Mason. Mason was a great drinker; when drunk Mason had beaten him but he was loose-mouthed and had revealed many secrets, telling of his adventures in the Revolution, and how, when his daughter married, he had invited a great crowd to celebrate and then ordered his gang to waylay them. Mason had admitted that he had several subsidiary highwaymen operating separately but under his orders.

Circling again, it was Mason's turn to talk. Yes, he had held Setton captive, and sometimes by force; he had hung onto him because he knew the man to be guilty of many crimes for which he himself had been wrongfully accused. Thus the Owsley robbery, and many murders along the Trace: he had held Setton, hoping that some day he might trick the man into a public confession, to clear his own fair name.

So in the little log cabin courthouse, through the chill January days, the strange ring-around-a-rosy game of lies continued. Mason had told Setton that he had fifty highwaymen at his call. Setton had told Mason that if he were ever pursued he could summon a troop of five hundred Choctaw braves to defend him. And the son, John Mason: his father had always tried to "live a decent life"; Setton was the villain.

But by now the judges had heard enough. On January 31, 1803, they finally directed that "the proceedings of this trial, originally set down in writing on 91 sheets of paper written on both sides, as well as the pieces of evidence tending to conviction, together with seven thousand piasters in United States banknotes, be forwarded to the Honorable Governor General by Don Robert McCoy, Captain of the Militia, whom we have charged to conduct the prisoners, Mason and consorts, to New Orleans with the view of their trial being continued and finished, if it so please the Honorable Governor General."

They started down the River—the Captain, his interpreter, a guard of five men, Setton, the four Masons, the woman, the three children: it was a crowded boatload, and the trip took two full weeks; one can picture them, sullen, venomous, split apart by hatred and hedged round with rifles, drifting to their destiny down the lazy-rolling River.

They came to New Orleans; the High Court reviewed the case. The High Court decided that since all the crimes of which they severally and together stood accused had been committed on American soil they should be turned over to the courts of the Mississippi territory for trial. At the beginning of March, 1803, they were carried aboard a small sailing sloop, and the journey upriver to Natchez began.

The weather was stormy; turbulent currents and a wind that came clapping down in gusts from every quarter combined to delay them. They were almost a month on the way and still they were more than a hundred miles south of Natchez, and here—abreast the little river town of Pointe Coupée—fate touched them.

A townsman saw it all, saw through the rain and

the gray water the little sloop tossing and churning, saw her luff into the wind and then, caught by the next gust, heel over terribly, saw the sails crack and the mast splinter: "The mast of their vessel broke, a part of their men were sent on shore to make a new one, and the rest were left to guard the prisoners. In a short time they threw off their irons, seized the guns belonging to the boat and fired upon the guards. Captain McCoy hearing the alarm ran out of the cabin, old Mason instantly shot him through the breast and shoulder; he with the determined bravery of a soldier, though scarcely able to stand, shot him in the head. Mason fell and rose, fell and rose again, and although in a gore of blood, one of his party having shot a Spaniard's arm to pieces, he drove off McCoy's party and kept possession of the boat till evening." But by now the landsmen had been drummed into a boarding party; a dozen skiffs set out to attack them: "Discovering a superior force they left the boat, the women and children following with great precipitation. There is a party of Caroles after them and it is supposed they will succeed in taking them. The Commandant at this place has offered one thousand dollars for taking old Mason dead or alive. They will be pursued with the utmost diligence by a set of determined fellows."

The escape had been made on March 26, 1803; in spite of all pursuit, for more than six months longer the veteran highwayman resisted capture. In June, he was sighted, armed to the teeth, by a party of travelers along the Trace; after an exchange of shots, he disappeared. In July, a stranger named James Mays (but undoubtedly the Samuel Mays who rode away at Henry Havard's death) appeared in Natchez to report that he had been held up and robbed by Mason, on the Trace.

He procured fresh supplies and plunged into the wilderness again, in search of the bandit. And now the woods were alive with searchers; men, blood-hounds, Indians everywhere went crashing here and there through the thicket: it seemed no man could elude them but Mason did. And in October Mays came toiling back to Natchez. With him was the man Setton; he was arrested at sight, and Mays with him. Both were clapped in jail but speedily freed again, and now Setton had guaranteed to guide Mays to Mason's hide-out, and help to capture him. They set out together in a canoe, crossing toward the Louisiana side.

They came back within the month, with a large lumpy ball of clay, dried hard, in the bow of the canoe. They had found the bandit hiding in the swampy area around Lake Concordia, west of Natchez. Setton's presence had disarmed old Mason's suspicions; they had joined him, helped him cook his meal, sat with him afterward around the fire; that night they had tomahawked him, cut off his head. "They took Mason's head back to Natchez in the bow of a canoe, rolled up in blue clay, to prevent putrefaction." How else could they prove his death and claim the reward?

Before the magistrates at Natchez they broke the clay ball open and revealed its gruesome burden. Mason was dead. Where was the money? In the midst of the parleying, a stranger burst into the room: he had recognized, among their horses, two that had been stolen from him some time before. Hardly had the inquiry into this matter been started when another stranger, a Captain Stump from Kentucky, moved closer to Setton, staring. "Why, that man's Wiley Harpe!" he said.

Until now, no report of the findings at New Madrid, as to the identity of Mason's mysterious partner, had reached Natchez. Here was news indeed. To be sure, Captain Stump had been none too certain in his identification: under Setton's indignant protests he had wavered, said that he couldn't be absolutely sure. The suspect was put under double guard, and proclamations were posted at the inns, along the waterfront: let any man who had known Little Harpe, and could identify him, come to the town jail, where one was held suspected to be he.

Several boatmen appeared. "That's Harpe all right," they said. He denied it. But at last a man

The End of Mason

named John Bowman, from Knoxville, Tennessee, made identification absolute: "If he's Little Harpe, he'll have a scar under the left nipple of his breast, because I cut him there in a little difficulty we had, one night at Knoxville." Harpe, still bluffing, protested but they tore off his shirt: the scar was there.

They escaped, and were almost immediately recaptured in the town of Greenville, some twenty miles north of Natchez, and there, finally, they were tried and convicted. On February 8, 1804, they were led from the jail and out through the town to the "Gallows-Field," to be hanged.

In the general custom, condemned prisoners would be driven to the field in a wagon, with their coffin for a seat on the way. Still in the wagon, the noose that hung from a beam between two forked trees would be fitted around their necks; then the driver would give a "Gee-up!" to his horses; the wagon would move away beneath their feet and the men would swing there, hanged.

In the case of Harpe and Mays, however, for some reason the procedure varied: they walked to the Gallows-Field with their hands tied behind their backs; under the noose, a ladder was braced: they were forced to climb it till their necks came under the rope. They stood there a moment—Harpe sullen, wordless to the last; Mays, protesting: "Mays com-

163

plained of the hardship of his fate, said he had not been guilty of crimes deserving death and spoke of the benefit he had rendered society by destroying old Mason"—in the midst of it, the ladder was knocked away, and they swung there until they were dead, hanged.

After the execution, their heads were cut off. The head of Harpe was mounted on a pole along the Trace, a little north of the town; the head of Mays was mounted on a pole and placed a little south of the town, along the Trace. Their bodies were buried in the town graveyard but at this a furor arose: families whose relatives had been buried there protested at such company. The night after the burial, they came with picks and shovels, dug up their own dead and carried them away to a field beyond the town and buried them again.

It was as well that they did so. In a few years, as the Trace widened and deepened under heavier traffic, it encroached on the old graveyard along whose borders it ran. Wagon wheels, horses' hooves, rutting the soil, wore open the shallow graves of Little Harpe and Samuel Mays. The day came when a teamster's dog, burrowing, dragged out the crumbling bones and scattered them; when the graves became only two ruts crosswise on the road, in which the heavy wheels bounced or the horses' hooves stumbled among whitish splintered fragments mixed indiscriminately with the dust; when finally, by the rains and the roadmenders' shovels, and the grind of traffic, the surface of the way was leveled off again and even the last vestiges of the burying place of the two bandits were obliterated.

"I have carried off more than a thousand slaves."
—*A print from "The Life and Adventures of John A. Murrell."*

"They took the body, one by the heels and one by the head, and heaved it out over the edge of the ravine."
—*A print from*
"The Life and Adventures of John A. Murrell."

IV
MURREL

A MAN IN A BOLIVAR COAT

ON JUNE 1, 1833, a young man named Virgil Stewart set out from the town of Jackson, Tennessee: he had sold his farm and a brace of negro field hands; he had turned the cash into trade goods—bolted calico, bullet molds, cutlery, tin ware—and he was heading south into the newly opened territory of the "Choctaw Purchase."

This was that belt of swamp and canebrake, stretching across the northern half of the state of Mississippi, which had in the earlier years formed so dangerous a barrier to traffic along the Natchez Trace. Mason had hidden there; Hare and the Harpes had made it their headquarters: hunted over by the Indians and haunted by highwaymen, it had remained dark and treacherous still, while to north and south of it the towns were springing up and the forest being cleared away.

But now even this last outpost of the wilderness was to be cleared and cultivated. Old General Coffee had made a treaty with the Choctaw chieftains: the Indians had ceded the land and moved out west of the Mississippi: in the Fall of the year, at the town of Chocchuma, a great land sale would be held, to open the region to settlers. Young Stewart had decided to get down there early.

He was a Georgian by birth but he had always been a wanderer. His father had died early; his mother had left him to shift for himself; he had drifted westward, working from plantation to plantation, until finally he had landed in Jackson and settled there.

He was a good-looking young fellow, well set up, blond, blue-eyed, and with a hardy cast of countenance. He had seen hard going and he had learned to keep a tight jaw but he knew how to make friends: in Jackson old Parson John Henning and his wife had been almost father and mother to him. Henning had lent him money to get his farm going and Stewart was grateful to him, yet even the Hennings had not been able to argue him out of his determination to move into the new country. He was a stubborn determined young man at bottom.

He made his way south, by flatboat and mulepack, peddling his goods along the way. He still had a considerable supply on hand when, early in July, he reached the town of Tuscahoma in the Purchase, where he planned to spend the summer. He decided to take his stock to the general store at the settlement and sell out.

The storekeeper at Tuscahoma was Edward Clanton, and he was quite willing to strike a bargain. He took Stewart's goods and gave him credit for

A Man In A Bolivar Coat

their value; furthermore, Stewart agreed to tend store for Clanton, in return for his board and lodging.

It developed that Clanton was away a good deal, on business trips through the territory, and Stewart was left pretty much in full charge of the store but it never occurred to him to question that. And Clanton was very agreeable: he introduced the young man to a most friendly couple, a Mr. William Vess and his wife. Soon an arrangement had been made for Stewart to board with the Vess family, instead of at Clanton's bachelor cabin.

So the life of the small community grew up around him and enfolded him. Clanton was a rich man, as the town knew riches—beside the store, he owned a large plantation, and an unconscionable number of slaves—and his friendship was helpful to the young man. Vess was of different caliber: he was a journeyman carpenter by trade but he was a lazy one and little inclined to stay on the job. He would vanish for days at a time, and reappear again to talk vaguely of "projects" and sprawl in the sun on the doorstep.

Mrs. Vess was a bouncing woman, red-haired, with an almost truculent heartiness of manner. But she was kind to Stewart—sometimes he felt that there was a hint of something more than kindness in her approaches—and she was an excellent cook. It was hard to understand where the money came from, with Vess so shiftless, and yet their table was always plentiful.

They even had coffee with every meal, and coffee —real coffee—in those times was a luxury. Most of the settlers served it only for Sunday morning breakfast, and brewed concoctions of Evans root or dried pea-pods the rest of the time. But Mrs. Vess couldn't put up with makeshifts.

"I like a good cup of coffee, and there's nothing else'll do," she said. And when Stewart came in from the store at sundown she always had a potful waiting for him, along with a platter of hoe cake and dodger cake, a rasher of bacon, plenty of eggs, broilings of hung beef and maybe a cup of custard for the evening meal.

So, when the land sales fell due at Chocchuma in the fall, Stewart didn't bother to bestir himself. He was now, tacitly or otherwise, a partner in Clanton's store, and business, with the inrush of homesteaders, was booming: he was quite satisfied where he was. Winter set in, the dull and dreary, rainy season of the year. True to the native superstition that a hog will root out and kill a rattler, he helped Vess herd his pigs down to the snake-infested lower pasture; he helped him hive in the other cattle. Finally, toward January, he decided to pay a visit to his friends, the Hennings, up in Jackson.

Clanton said he could spare him; Mrs. Vess fixed

A Man In A Bolivar Coat

him a snack of hoe cake and bacon for his saddle bags and bantered him about the pretty girls he would meet along the way; Vess grinned and spat, shuffled his feet and said nothing. On January 18, 1834, young Stewart was riding north again along the Natchez Trace, into Tennessee. Not in his wildest surmise could he have guessed the terrible mission that lay before him, nor the changed condition that awaited his return.

He arrived in Jackson a week later, toward evening; he rode directly to the Hennings' cabin; he was not long in discerning that a certain preoccupation clouded the welcome the old couple gave him. After he had been fed, and the puncheon table cleared of its platters, the cause of their worry was made clear.

Someone was stealing the parson's niggers. One had been stolen some time ago, and now two more, prime field hands both, had vanished in the past week. A good working negro was worth, in those days, anywhere from seven hundred to a thousand dollars; the loss was serious. Henning had not the cash to buy others, and he was too old to work in the fields himself: he was beginning to wonder where he was going to turn.

Stewart stared, and then at the thought of the kindly old couple thus brought so close to ruin his heart began to pound a little: he'd like to lay hands

173

on the robber, he thought. "Well," he demanded, "who d'ye think got them?"

Henning shook his head slowly. "I ain't no idea," he muttered, but his wife interrupted. "You have so, John, and you know it!" she cried.

The old man remonstrated: he would rather lose ten times the value of the slaves than accuse an innocent person, he said, but she was at the end of her patience. "I'll say it if you won't," she cried. "It's that slick deceiving rascal Murrel!"

And now the story came out. There was no fact, no definite circumstance on which they could base their accusation; it was still a matter of suspicion only, but backed by observation of the equivocal activities, the furtive comings and goings of the man.

Murrel was a recent settler in the region. He had come—and hints of doubtful doings had come with him—from somewhere down near Memphis. He had a wife and a younger brother, but no children; he had bought land and opened up a big farm, and he lived there royally.

He was evidently a man with almost a passion for magnificence. When he rode—and he was always riding out on some mysterious mission of his own—it was on the finest specimens of horseflesh obtainable; his clothes were tailored down the River in New Orleans; his boots and his hats he bought in Philadelphia. All this—and his air of wealth, his

free-handedness with his money, the plausible gallant prideful way he had—gave him a certain weight
in the community: there were many who swore by
him and courted him. And yet, even to these,
there was something about the man that was faintly
repellent.

He was too well dressed: he was too much the
type of "modern dandy" that old Judge Breazeàle
was railing against, "with his superfine cloth pantaloons strapped on at both extremities of his person,
his shirt fastened with tape, ribbons and gold buttons, a superfine cloth coat upon his back, a dandy
silk hat with a rim three-quarters inches wide upon
his head, and right and left calf-skin boots upon his
feet." He was too handsome, with his smooth sallow
cheeks, his sleek dark hair, and his wide eyes always
lit as if with some inner ironic meaning. He carried
his head high but there was something in the pose
that suggested a snake about to strike and there was
always about him a faint imponderable hint of evil,
like the effluvium that is supposed to emanate from a
poisonous reptile. In spite of his many friends—and
many of these were vaguely suspect—the Hennings
were not alone in doubting him.

And Murrel had learned of this. "He wrote me
a letter," Parson Henning explained. It was a flowery affair, written after the orotund manner of the
day: he spoke of his "long and earnestly continued

friendship," deprecated their suspicions, insisted that all his activities were "clear and open as the day." He stated that he was leaving on January 25 for a business trip to Randolph, Tennessee, a town just north of Memphis on the Mississippi, but on his return he would welcome their fullest investigation.

Stewart sat with the Hennings, studying the situation, wondering how he could grapple with this strange man. He.had, he noted, one great advantage: Murrel, so far, had no knowledge of him at all. This advantage, he also saw, could be held only so long as he kept himself invisible in the town; there were many older settlers who would remember him and his friendship for the Hennings, and Murrel would inevitably be put on the alert. And so in the end it was decided that Stewart would lie hidden in Henning's cabin through the next two days, and when on the twenty-fifth Murrel rode out on his trip to Randolph, Stewart would intercept him, trace where he went or, better still, try to win his confidence and learn his secret. Young Stewart was blossoming forth as a detective.

The morning of January twenty-fifth dawned clear and cold. The better to cover his movements, Stewart had ridden down the night before to Denmark, a small town about four miles west along the trail Murrel would follow. And now, hardly after

A Man In A Bolivar Coat

the first birds were peeping, he set out, riding slowly, waiting for his man to overtake him.

He reached the settlement of Estanaula, and here there was a toll bridge across the Big Hatchee River; here he halted. "Do you know a man named Murrel from up by Jackson?" he asked the toll gate tender. Yes, the gateman knew him; Murrel often passed that way. "Well, when he passes to-day I want you to point him out to me, but don't let him know about it."

Stewart waited. There was not much traffic along the Trace. Occasionally a traveler would come riding up, his horse's hoofs ringing with the clear sharp sound they have in frosty weather; he would pay his toll, go clattering across the loose-planked roadway of the bridge, and vanish down the trail. After each had passed, Stewart looked questioningly at the gate tender and the other shook his head. No, that was not Murrel.

But then at last another man came riding, a handsome man with the glossiest beaver hat slanted over his insolent eyes, and a wide-skirted coat, fastidiously cut, well brushed and immaculate, buttoned tightly about his form. A brace of silver-mounted pistols showed at his saddle holsters, and his horse's flanks steamed and quivered as he drew rein at the toll gate, tossed a coin to the tender, and spurred on again.

177

The Outlaw Years

When this jaunty rider had crossed the bridge, the gateman turned to Stewart. "That's Murrel," he said. "The man in the Bolivar coat."

Stewart caught up with him a mile or two down the Trace. He gave him good morning. Murrel answered courteously—he had a clipping, "high-toned" way of speaking—but his manner indicated a certain aloofness, as if to discourage further advances. Stewart, however, persisted: "Cold day for riding," he went on and, distantly, Murrel agreed.

Stewart played the game as he had planned it. He overflowed with confidences. "Lost a horse," he explained, "or more likely 'twas stole, I reckon. Anyways, I'm out to find it."

Murrel turned an enigmatical eye on him, and for a moment Stewart felt a cold quiver of doubt at his heart. The man had the flat pale glance of a killer.

But he answered non-committally: there was a good deal of robbing and rascality going on hereabouts, Murrel ventured.

Stewart assented. "There sure is, stranger!" he cried. "And I don't know as how I can blame them. Why, look here!" he argued. "The times is that hard, and it's such a tight squeak for a fellow to make his living that if he sees a prime piece of horseflesh and is sharp enough to seize on to it, why I say he deserves it. Always excepting," and he slapped his

178

thigh and laughed, "when the horse happens to be my own!" He noted that Murrel's face was relaxing in a smile as well.

"There are some slick ones about," said Murrel. "Right here in Tennessee there is a company of rogues so sharp that nothing can be done about them."

Stewart held his line; he was getting surer of his ground. Rogues? He objected: was the rich man a rogue when he flooded a whole county with worthless currency? Was the boomer a rogue when he sold out a township in sites at ten times the land's value? No; the only rogue was the poor man, and for his own part he held it all to be the rankest injustice. "Sir, my doctrine is, let the hardest fend off!"

"It is the law that settles all these matters," Murrel remarked sententiously. "Let a man learn the use of the law, and nothing can touch him." He hesitated, stroking his chin, while the two horses jingled onward, flank to flank. Doubtless he knew that he ought to say no more about such matters but he was a vain man, proud of his own shrewdness, and here was this baby-faced youngster gaping at him: he could not resist some slight parading—where was the harm, if he spoke in the third person always? His face loosened in that fatuous deprecative grin that oils a man's mouth when he tells of his own triumphs and Stewart, watching, knew that he had his man hooked at last. Flattery was all the bait he needed; thenceforward on that long strange journey Stewart admired and Murrel expanded—and ruined himself in the process.

As they rode, Stewart made notes of the conversation. He scratched names and dates with a pin on his saddle-skirts; whenever they halted and he could find means to be alone for a moment he would write down all Murrel had told him on the pages of a blank-book he carried in his pocket. In the end, he had a sort of scenario recounting, episode by episode, the man's whole criminal career as it moved toward the planned culmination, his dream of a pirate empire in the West.

It was toward the climax of that plot that he was then riding and even as he rode, step by step, he betrayed it. Only in the wilderness could so mad a scheme have been conceived or its recital have been plausible, and so it is against that dark background, like horsemen on a frieze, that we must picture them, as the slow tale unfolded.

They rode cautiously. "The weather was very cold and the road much cut up and then hard frozen, and covered with sleet. It was bad traveling and they got on but slow." Murrel's beginning was equally cautious. "Now, there is that company of hellions I spoke of," he began. He told of the two brothers—"keen, shrewd fellows"—who were at its head. "The eldest brother is one of the best judges of law in the United States. They all work under him, robbing and stealing, and he paves the way for them so that the law can never reach them."

A slick one, said Stewart, admiring: that's a man to make his way in the world!

"You are right, sir! Why, he has stolen more niggers than you could count, and always got off with it." He told how, not long since, he had been caught with three niggers sworn to belong to a neighbor named Long. "They took him before an old fool of a squire that had vowed to convict him, and the people all thought he was good for the penitentiary, but he laughed at them: it was only a finable offense, he told them, and they could make the most of it and be damned to them!

"Well, sir, when Court-day come the house was thronged to hear it. He had employed the most eminent lawyer at the bar, Andrew L. Martin, but during the evidence he took his lawyer aside and cursed him. 'Damn you!' says he. 'I pay you my money and now I must show you how to work!' He gave him hell, and he got him into the way of the law. Martin is a flowery fellow, but he has not dived into the quirks of the trade like his client."

Finding they could not jail him, the citizens had

taken other measures: "They formed a company, which they called Captain Slick's company, and advertized for all honest men to meet at the schoolhouse to bind themselves against him. But he could read their notices as well as any, and he got some of his own strong friends into the company, and they told him when to make ready.

"So one night they came against him; there were over two dozen among them, but he had got together an immense quantity of guns and ammunition, and he had eighteen friends with him, primed for an engagement. He had prepared his house and outbuildings with portholes and placed his men with the skill of a general. So they marched up, and took one look, and they marched off again, and a fine thing for them they did, for he was situated to cut them all down! And the law would have upheld him, too!"

Stewart was all gapes and stares. A man of wonderful talent, he exclaimed. Such a man might be a general or a statesman, if the country knew how to use him.

Murrel's eyes narrowed. "He may yet be a general," he announced darkly. "And a statesman, too! He may surprise them all!" he burst out. They had slowed to a rambling walk, but now he pricked his horse and started suddenly ahead, stiff and tense in the saddle, as if the force of his own passion had

A Man In A Bolivar Coat

swept him forward. Stewart, amazed, trotted after him down the trail.

Murrel slowed soon; his smile was gone. He was suspicious. "How might your name be?" he demanded. Stewart told him, Hues—Adam Hues. He said he was from down on the Yalo Busha River, in the Purchase; he told a pretty straight story. Murrel relaxed a little. And they rode along—the wintry sun rose high but its light was white and chill, there was no warmth in it, and now a cold raw wind came to press against their faces; though Murrel gave no heed, Stewart was numbed by it: he pulled out a flask of brandy to warm him, and shared it with the other—and soon Murrel was talking again.

A man was a fool not to know the law, he said. "There ain't a dozen men in the Valley that know the law," he declared. "The Judges? All they know is what they can read in the 'Justice's Form Book,' and any other man can do the same. I've seen them all. Old Judge Haywood up in Nashville—he lays around all day on a bull's hide under a tree, and he's so fat it takes three niggers dragging at the tail to haul him into the shade—what's he know about the law? A smart man could tie him into knots!"

Like this elder brother they were talking about, Stewart suggested. Murrel assented warmly: "He

183

has discovered a point or two that he uses to advantage," he admitted.

Stewart asked: "What age is this wonderous man you speak of?"

And Murrel: "He is about thirty, I suppose, and his brother just grown up; he is a smart fellow too, but not half the experience of the elder. I will tell you of one of his routes on a speculation a few months passed, and you can judge of his talents. . . ."

They had topped a rise, and looked down on the scattered cabins of a tiny settlement, set in the thickly wooded valley. The smoking chimneys showed how snug it must be within doors and the thought only made them more cold and miserable: "The smoke from the cabins had settled among the heavy timber of an extensive bottom in large black columns, as if the trees were wrapped in mourning. . . ." They went clattering down the trail and along the frozen road between the houses. No one appeared to hail them: "all were closely housed, and around the fire." They rode on, into the forest again.

Murrel was recounting the exploits of the mysterious "elder brother." Running off slaves, for instance: he told how he had figured to beat the law in that. Stealing a nigger would be a prison offense, but he was too shrewd: he persuaded the niggers to run off of their own free will, and then he would hide them, waiting until the owner advertised a reward.

"Now, sir, that advertisement amounts to the same as a power of attorney, to take his property, the nigger, and hold it for him. And if a man chooses to make a breach of trust in this case, and instead of carrying the nigger to the owner converts him to his own use—why, that is not stealing, and the only way the owner can get at him is in a civil action." And this shrewd fellow cared nothing for a lawsuit: he owned no property; all his funds were in cash.

Murrel leaned over, grinning, and gave Stewart a jog with his elbow: "And who do you think owns the bank where he keeps his cash? Why, one of his own clan, that would stand with him no matter what happens!"

"His clan . . ." Stewart was to remember that. He had heard rumors. . . .

Murrel went rattling on. This shrewd elder brother sold his niggers time and time again: sometimes he would make as much as three or four thousand dollars out of one of them. But, Stewart objected, each time the nigger ran off, there would be rewards out for him, with descriptions: in the end, the whole Valley would be looking for him, and what then?

The Outlaw Years

Murrel leaned close again, with a thin smile on his lips and his eyes hard. "There is an easy way of getting rid of a nigger, when he is likely to be recognized," he said. Once, coming north along the Trace, this sharp fellow had sold a stolen nigger to a settler. He got six hundred dollars for the boy, and that very night he met the nigger, as he had directed, under a China-tree in the lane beyond the plantation and carried him off again.

It was quick work, but the previous owners were after him: he hurried on up the Trace to the home of a friend of his—"a rich man and well respected, but one of the clan, nevertheless"—he hid the nigger and felt safe there.

But next day, in the town tavern, he saw a placard, advertising the boy as a runaway and describing himself as the probable thief: they were hot after him. "It was squally times, and any port in a storm. He took the nigger out on the bank of a creek which ran by the farm of his friend and shot him through the head. So he got rid of him."

But the body, asked Stewart; how did he get rid of the body?

"Oh! That is easy. He cuts open the belly and scrapes out the guts, and then fills him up with sand and throws him into the river to feed the eels. . . ." The trail had dipped through a grove of poplars; the sun was setting, and its red glow reflected a

186

dim light that was more like a haze, rosy and pal-
pable, from the white-stemmed trees, now whiter
still with their glaze of frost. Murrel stopped talking suddenly and drew rein; he sat staring. "That is
a beautiful scene," he remarked.

Night fell: they rode by moonlight with every
bare branch in the forest around them glistening in
its sleety casing.

"Did you ever travel much by moonlight?" Murrel asked.

"Not much, sir."

"It is the best time, sir."

And again—Stewart had dropped behind: a wave
of apprehension had suddenly gripped him and he
rode, fingering his pistol, staring at the other's back
—Murrel turned, all unconscious, and beckoned him
forward: "Come, sir, ride up. I have a friend farther
on who will give us a bed for the night, but it is
some way to go, and we had best pass the time as
lively as possible. I will tell you another feat of
this elder brother."

He told how shrewd the man was at deception.
"He is tall and well proportioned. He is a damned
imposing fellow. Sometimes he goes dressed in the
Methodist order. He is well versed in Scriptures
and preaches a hell of a fine sermon." After the

preaching, it was easy to pass off counterfeit money on the congregation.

They stayed that night at the friend's house. Stewart, worn out, dragged himself wearily up the ladder to the loft and went to bed immediately: as he dozed, he heard the two men—Murrel and his friend—talking softly in the room below. Next day, Murrel rose before him: "Murrel rose very early and had the horses caught and saddled, ready for a start by clear daylight." They rode on again.

And as yesterday the talk had been of robbery only, now it was of murder: it was as if the man had unbuttoned his sleek outer coat, opening it on the bloody garments underneath. Now at last Stewart was seeing the assassin in all the cold nakedness of his intent, and it sickened him.

This elder brother—it was dangerous to cross him. He had friends everywhere. His confederates robbed on the River and on the Trace, and he took a share of revenue from all of them. He had friends in high places, too. Once, traveling down-river with a stolen slave, a gambler informed on him to the Captain, who seized the nigger. But when they reached New Orleans he got his friends to go to the Mayor, and before you knew it the nigger was loose and the Captain was in jail. "And as for the Captain's pretty friend who knew so much, he soon had a nurse that tended him day and night, until he found his way to the bottom of the River. . . ."

Murrel turned suddenly. "Look here! I am going over to Arkansaw, and why don't you come along with me?"

But Stewart was looking for his horse.

"Damn the horse! It's a cross-and-pile chance at best that you ever find him. Let him go to hell! A man with as keen an eye as yours should never spend his time hunting after a damned horse!"

But Stewart hadn't money enough for the trip.

"I will let you have money if you give out. I have thousands of friends over there; it will not cost us a cent if we stay six months, and I'll guarantee you a better horse than the one you're hunting. I'll learn you a few tricks if you come with me!"

Stewart said he would consider it, and yet as he spoke, he knew with a sick certainty that there was only one possible answer he could make. He must keep on. He could not stop. The invitation, in the moment he refused it, would become a command: Murrel would not let him leave now. He knew too much.

Stewart said he would decide in the morning.

That night they stayed at a roadside inn: "The place will never be forgot by Hues.

"So soon as they were warm they were lit to their lodgings. It was in a large open room, and the bed tick was stuffed with corn shucks, which made as much noise when they got in, as riding a new saddle. The covering consisted of a thin cover-lid, and cotton counterpane.

"Murrel lay and cursed the landlord all night, and Hues lay and shivered like he had a hard ague until morning.

"Next morning Murrel inquired for the bill— it was 12-pence each, for the lodging. 'What!' says Murrel. 'A 'leven-penny bit for riding such a colt as we rode last night? He has not been curried since the day he was foaled. Damned high for lodging in the shuck pen!' "

They had hardly started before Murrel, with his cool easy smile of limitless assurance, put the question: "Well, Mr. Hues, what say you of the trip to Arkansaw this morning?"

The decisive moment had come, and still Stewart hesitated. "I have not fairly determined of the matter, but I think I will go."

"Go? Yes, damn it, you must go! I will make a man of you."

"That is what I want, sir."

"There is some of the handsomest girls over there you ever saw. I am in town when I am there!"

A Man In A Bolivar Coat

"Nothing to object to, sir. I am quite partial to handsome ladies."

"Oh! Well, go with me to Arkansaw, and damn me if I don't put you right in amongst them, and they are as plump as ever come over, sir!"

They rode all morning. Toward noon Murrel remarked that they had made good time on the way: "We are within half a mile of Wesley. We will have a warm there."

Stewart answered vaguely: they might eat at the tavern, he said . . . buy some brandy. . . .

"We will get the brandy, but I have lots of provisions in my portmanteau," said Murrel.

The approach to the town of Wesley presented a new problem to the harassed Stewart. He had three very good friends there; he knew they would be sure to hail him: "They would divulge his proper name and appear suspicious to Murrel, for Murrel believed him in a country where he was known to no person, and in all probability one of them would begin to inquire about his friends in Madison county, who lived within 5 miles of Murrel's house, and so the whole matter would be upset. . . ." It was a ticklish situation, but the mention of the brandy had given him an idea.

They rode on. They were entering the town. Stewart reined in. "Is that sign the tavern, sir?" he asked.

"Yes, sir, that is the Wesley Inn. We can warm there."

But Stewart had another suggestion. He had made up his mind to go to Arkansaw, he said, but first he must see after his missing horse. He would stop at the general store which he noticed a little way down from the inn, and post a notice and a reward for the horse; meantime, the other might go on to the inn, get the brandy, and wait for him there.

Murrel agreed. "Do your writing quick, and come on to the tavern," he said. "I will see to the fire there the first thing I do." He cantered off.

Stewart hurried on to the store; it was owned by one of his friends and had, he knew, the only license to sell retail liquor in the town. Here he learned that two of his friends were out of town. There remained only Colonel Bayliss, who they told him was sitting in the tavern.

Stewart slipped into the street again and ducked behind a paling. He was in time to see Murrel stroll out of the inn and start across the road toward the store: as Stewart expected, he had asked for brandy at the tavern and had been told that he must buy it at the store. As soon as he was out of sight, Stewart dashed for the inn.

"He found Colonel Bayliss in a back room, and apprized him of his designs, so that the Colonel passed him as a stranger while in the presence of Murrel"; in addition, he borrowed a pistol from Bayliss and tucked it in his waistband beside his own. He felt safer now.

When Murrel returned, he found his friend Hues seated calmly beside the fire in the inn-common, toasting his boots at the fender. They had a glass together, and then they were out on the road again. Murrel rode silently now.

He seemed ill at ease; he twisted about in the saddle to peer back along the trail. At last, at a bend in the trail, he spurred suddenly into the forest. Stewart felt for his pistol grip—he had no idea what this strange man's next move might be—and followed blindly.

Murrel led him to a clearing, well hidden from the trail. Here they dismounted. "We'll have a bite of cold victuals," said Murrel.

He pulled a slab of jerked beef from his saddle bag; they sat side by side on a fallen log, hacking at the meat with their case-knives, chewing huge mouthfuls. Murrel took a swig at the bottle and looked with a grinning eye at his companion.

"Well, Hues, I will be damned if I can't put you in a better business than trading with the Indians," he said.

Stewart said he had no doubt of it.

"Did you ever hear," asked Murrel, grinning

broader still, "of those devils, the Murrels, up in Madison County, in this state?"

Stewart—he knew now what was coming—replied that he was an entire stranger to them.

"Well, sir," said Murrel. "I might as well out with it. I am that elder brother I have been telling you of!"

SUCH GENTEEL MANNERS

MASON, HARE and the Harpes were all dead and much of the wild bitter spirit that had animated them was dead too. In the early days men had lived hived in their narrow cabins like animals in a lair, and the early riders of the Trace had robbed, fought passionately, killed, with the same fierce unpremeditated animal intensity. It had been a dark time; every gesture men made had been as if pregnant with strange menaces and at last, in 1812, war was born of their strivings.

It came at the sign of a comet in the sky, and with the forewarning of earthquakes, driving families in terror from their houses, while "the earth quivered like a fallen beef that has been shot through the brain." It lasted two years and when it ended men awoke with a sudden exhilaration to a sense of new freedom. All the fears that had oppressed them—of the Spaniard, the Englishman, the Indian —existed no longer. The Valley was free to grow, to spread out, to expand in every direction, and people went about clapping each other on the shoulder, as if intoxicated by the limitless possibilities of the nation.

The Outlaw Years

Politically, it was the "era of good feeling" and the same tolerance extended into the social aspect of life as well. A drunken man never bothers to count his change: every man he meets is his friend and a good fellow, and the Valley was drunk with its golden expectations, dizzy with huge prospects: it could even grin good-naturedly at the sharp fellows who picked its present pocket.

It was a queer time. Ladies whose sole idea of literature had been drawn from the pages of Burgh's "Dignity of Human Nature" or Fanny Burney's "Evelina"—borrowed from the score or so of books in the Coonskin Library—now sent their daughters to Miss Allison's High School for Young Ladies at New Orleans, or to Mrs. Wilkinson's French Academy at Cincinnati, where they learned "Good Order and Propriety" at meals, and were taught French, Sewing, the Analysis of Participles and the Lessons of Morality: terms, $50 quarterly, paid in advance.

Everybody was hot after culture. Young maidens struggled with charcoal pencil and drawing paper, composed mournful "elegies," laboriously knotted stray strands of hair into wreaths, spider-webs, lace garlands and pasted them in huge "hair albums," made scissor silhouettes in hopeless emulation of that consummate genius Miss Honeywell, who possessed "the rare talent of executing with a common pair of scissors, by holding them in her mouth, every object in nature or art with the greatest ease to herself." Miss Honeywell's "Gallery of Cuttings" was everywhere a sell-out, at the admission of a shilling apiece, including a profile cut by the artist herself, but then everybody was going to lectures.

It was a rich time for quacks and charlatans of all description, and the mountebanks came pouring to profit by it. A generation earlier, people had believed that Seneca Oil was a sure cure for rheumatism and skunk oil for colds; that if a rattlesnake bit you on the leg you must hold the injured member higher than the head "so that the swelling would ascend"; that the sulphur water of Yellow Springs on the Little Miami was a panacea for all ailments, as witness the case of the Kentucky lady who had even been cured of cancer by imbibing the waters (or rather nearly cured, for "she was hurried away too soon by her friends, who lived a considerable distance away": as a result of this precipitancy the lady had died) and that the same water, if distilled off, left a residue which might be used to make an excellent paint, "equal to any Spanish brown"; that an expectant mother should drink plenty of Mississippi river-water to insure against a miscarriage.

And now they listened with the same credulity to the lectures of Webster the Mesmerist, Doctor Caldwell the Phrenologist, and watched in awed wonder while Signor Diego (known to Europe as The Great

Magician) descanted on the Hindu Miracles and demonstrated his "Wonderful Flight of a Young Lady, a Feat Never Before Attempted": tickets, 50 cents.

Mrs. Trollope toured through the valley, her small mind dazed by the exuberance she saw about her. Stopping at Cincinnati, she reported that "it was by no means a city of striking appearance; it wants domes, towers and steepels": she could not understand that to rear almost overnight a city of 20,000 population in the wilderness had been achievement enough, without bothering about beauty. When she rented a house for a season there, she was principally preoccupied with the fact that at parties ladies could expect lots of food but little attention from the men-folks, and that the city had no sewers at all!

She wondered what to do about her garbage. A delicate subject, but she finally appealed to a neighboring gentleman. "Why, just take it out in the middle of the street and dump it, ma'am. The pigs'll soon take it off," he told her. "But mind it's in the middle," he added, "for we have a law as forbids dumping such things at the side, to clutter up the walks." One can picture the tall Westerner, tolerantly eyeing the prim little busybody, with her strange questions.

And other towns lacked even more important

items than sewers. The pioneers had been content to clear a corn patch and live the labored life of the soil but the newcomers, the smart men, were too shrewd for that. They cleared townships and sold the sites. Sometimes they did not bother to clear the sites; sometimes they did not bother to build the towns: the climactic feat in townsite booming was perhaps that perpetrated by a genius whose name— or more probably his alias—was William Haddock.

A group of some fifty or sixty Easterners took passage on a packetboat down the Ohio: they wanted to be carried as near as possible to that thriving inland town of Rolling Stone. Curiously, none of the boatmen, it appeared, had ever heard of the place, and that was odd because, from all the evidence, it must be a busy and booming town indeed. The travelers displayed maps and circulars, which the agreeable gentleman who had sold them their townsites had given them. They displayed a splendid engraving, showing in "perspective view" the animated spectacle its Main Street presented at noonday. They even produced several copies of the town's weekly paper, the "Rolling Stone Messenger," its columns filled with items of the city's social doings and the feverish activities of its marts of trade.

The boatmen remained skeptical: there was no such town, they said, and all this ballyhoo was a fake. But the immigrants insisted and finally, having studied such maps as they had, the travelers were disembarked at the nearest point to where the town might possibly be. So they wandered off, the whole sad company, into the wilderness. It had been toward the close of a chill autumn; such supplies as they had brought were unseasonable and unpractical; winter closed in and they were still wandering, hunting vainly for the mythical township.

For it had all been a myth: the maps, the rich engravings, even the weekly "Messenger" with its plausible make-up had been part of a vast Gargantuan lie invented by the boomer, Mr. Haddock, to sell his town-lots. Some of the immigrants gave up the search; some others cleared land and settled; still others, worn out by cold and privation, died. Mr. Haddock went on, to sell more town-lots.

It was a rich time for the smart men. There had been an honesty—at least an openness of intention—in the old lawlessness, but now that the land was teeming with laws and lawyers legal dishonesty was the rule: "Accounts came from that sunny land of fussing, quarreling, murdering, violation of contracts and the whole catalog of *crimen falsi*. It was extolled as a legal Utopia." The courts were a mass of confusion: "They moved to quash everything. In one court, forthcoming bonds to the amount of some one hundred thousands of dollars were quashed because the execution was written 'State of Mississippi,' instead of 'The State of Mississippi.' "

Even in criminal cases, the same disorder was the rule: "Almost anything made out a case of self-defense—a threat—a quarrel—an insult—going armed, as almost all the wild fellows did—shooting from behind a corner, or out of the store door, in front or from behind—it was all self-defense."

As with the law, so with finance. Floods of worthless currency poured into the Valley; wild-cat bankers flourished. The procedure was simple: any one could procure a bank charter, issue currency, unload it in the settlements. In the end the profusion of these practically counterfeit notes almost cut off trade.

Clerks, cashiers and business men went armed with copies of the various Bank Note Detectors, such as that published by R. T. Bicknell in Philadelphia and advertised as "a handsome super royal sheet, published weekly at $2 per annum. The plan is to give the names and locations of all the Banks in the United States that are in credit, stating the discount on their notes at Philadelphia. To give also a list of all the broken banks, and a list of all the counterfeits known to be in circulation."

Consulting this, the harassed merchant would know at a glance which bills were worth a dime on the dollar, which were worthless, and which might be accepted at half, one-third or full value. But few customers would take these rulings tamely and most traders, to avoid dispute, preferred to carry their funds in gold. Which made matters simpler for the bandits who overtook them on the way.

For the bandits still persisted. Vast projects were constantly being unfolded for railroads that would cut the wilderness and span the continent, but men still traveled horseback, mule-pack along the Trace. As early as 1811, Zadock Cramer reported the experiments of "a Mr. Rosewalt, a gentleman of enterprise," with boats "propelled by the power of steam," and remarked that "it will be a novel sight, and as pleasing as novel, to see a huge boat working her way up the windings of the Ohio, without the appearance of sail, oar, pole or any manual labor about her—moving within the secrets of her own wonderful mechanism, and propelled by power undiscoverable!" And in the same year the steamer New Orleans was launched at Pittsburgh and made the journey, in spite of earthquake and hurricane, down-river to Natchez.

But it was to be many years before these primitive craft could carry much more than their own weight and a few cotton bales, and meantime the flatboat and the flatboatmen ruled the River as before—and all down the current the outlaws waited hived in their hiding-places, to pounce on the unwary.

Diamond Island was still a nest of brigands, as

Such Genteel Manners

it had been in the days of Kuykendall's courtship. Control of the Cave-in-Rock had been usurped by a most mysterious gentleman, named Philip Alston: "dressed in ruffles, broadcloth and lace," he went about the dirty business of scuttling Kentucky-boats and murdering their crews: he was supposed to have been a native of Natchez, of the bluest blue blood, and the tale goes that in the end, when his luck crashed, he escaped to Mexico and there rose again to high dignity—moving still among the Spanish gentlemen, courteously formal, dressed in his ruffles, broadcloth and lace.

He was succeeded at the Cave by a stouter character named Sturdevant, who lived surrounded by a small army of retainers: "He could, by blowing a horn, summon some fifty to a hundred armed men to his defense." He dealt in counterfeit money and did an immense business, selling one hundred dollars in bills at the rate of sixteen dollars, gold. The law at that time was only a vague conceit; justice was largely a matter of personal bias and expediency: it is typical of the nebulous ethics of the time that "the few farmers around, while not at all implicated in his crimes, rejoiced in the impunity with which he practiced his schemes." Sturdevant was a good fellow and a copious entertainer: his neighbors were little disposed to bother him.

Similarly, some distance down the river, James

The Outlaw Years

Ford for years combined the functions of Justice of the Peace, ferryman, and bandit chieftain. Even after the towns had arisen, and the conception of man's abstract civic duties had been formalized, Ford in his unique position succeeded in straddling the barrier between the lawless and the law-abiding, to his own profit. His ferry catered to travelers coming up along the northern extension of the Trace. His bandits robbed them. His court listened to their complaints. It was an unassailable position, and he held it with despotic rigor.

He was a tall man, "about six feet and very strong and broad." His head was large, and his features heavy: "On the whole, when in repose, he gives one the idea of a rather surly bull-dog." When aroused, he was a fury. His downfall came, not through interference from without, but through a split in his own gang. One of his pals, a man named Simpson, quarreled with him: Ford shot Simpson. A few nights later, "as he sat on the porch in his great arm-chair," one of his men approached with a note for him to read: to give him light, the fellow held a candle over his head. Thus illuminated, Ford made a perfect target: a confederate, hidden behind a rosebush in the yard, shot him dead.[1]

[1] A great mass of legend grew up, for some reason, about Ford and his activities. Many of his gang figure in tales of which most are familiar variants of ancient bandit dramas—the highwayman who kills his wife by mistake in a hold-up, the robber returning in disguise who is assassinated by his father and mother, etc. Ford's crimes became almost mythical

Such Genteel Manners

So, strung out along the Trace, the wilderness trails and the River, the bandits kept their strongholds safe. Once in a long while, a sporadic attempt would be made to oust some of the more flagrant offenders. Thus, in 1831, a party of Regulators was formed and descended on Sturdevant at the Cave, but were repulsed. Or again, a number of flatboatmen—all of whom had been attacked the previous year at the Crow's Nest, Mason's former headquarters in the Mississippi—banded their boats in fleet formation and fell upon the bandits there, and killed nineteen men in a savage battle upon the beach. But in general, the policy was "live and let live." It was a time of smart men and smart doings, and even among honest men, it was every man for himself.

The outlaws, in fact, in all that turbulent disordered time, were the sole class of men who retained their solidarity. There were invisible lines of communication through all the underworld, a network of common interest binding closer and closer all their

in grandeur: how he would fasten the head of an offending slave in a vise, and then burn out his eyes, tongue, nose; how he poisoned a friend to marry the friend's widow; how finally, when they came to bury him, the sky suddenly clouded, and it thundered heavily, and the Devil's hand reached up from the open grave and snatched Ford's coffin down to Hell straightway. Set against these, is the charming romance of Charles Webb, who escaped from a floatboat attacked by Ford's gang, dragged himself, wounded, to the bank, where he was found by Miss Cassandra Ford, daughter of the pirate: she carried him home with her, nursed him while he lay helpless in the robber stronghold, and at last, love having been born in both their hearts, eloped with him to the West, where they married and made their fortunes.

scattered hiding-places, and the gentlemen who strolled on Chartres Street in New Orleans, who bid in on the nigger jockeys at the Slave market on the Gallatin Road outside Nashville or bet on the flying mare Polly Medley at the races, who ferried across from Natchez to Vidalia, in the misty mornings or at sundown, to settle at the pistol's point their delicate affairs of honor, who preened and swaggered in the uneasy exercise of a new-found leisure—were pacing more narrowly near the edge of anarchy than they knew.

John A. Murrel was born in 1804. The exact place of his birth is uncertain: it is known only that it was in Tennessee, in the middle valley, and probably near the town of Columbia, some fifty miles south of Nashville on the Natchez Trace. His father was the proprietor of a small wayside tavern, and from this it might be deduced that the bandit had been born on the very highway he was later to terrorize, except that in equal likelihood his father's inn may have been located on that other trail which forked south from Columbia down to Fort Hamilton, or on still another, known formerly as the "Tennessee Path," which curved east and north through the Cumberlands to the Gap.

Of all this—his youth, his parentage, his birthplace—we have little more than his own random

Such Genteel Manners

reminiscences for information, as he chatted with Stewart on their ride together. It seemed that his father had been an industrious and decent citizen: "My father was an honest man, I expect"; he left the management of the inn in his wife's hands and she was of a different caliber entirely.

"My mother was of the pure girt: she learnt me and all her children to steal so soon as we could walk. At ten years old I was not a bad hand." Later, being clever and adroit, his mother made him her chief aide in her exploits: she herself, it would seem, was complaisant enough to linger occasionally in the traveler's chamber after lighting him to his room and after she had left and the exhausted guest was sleeping the son would come: he had developed a certain skill in opening locks. "The first good haul I made was from a peddler who lodged at my father's house one night. I had several trunk keys and I unlocked one of his trunks, and took a bolt of linen and several other things, and then locked the trunk." Next morning the boy waited apprehensively while the peddler loaded his packs but the man had not suspected: he rode off down the trail. Murrel, as he told the tale to Stewart, smiled at the memory of his youthful exploits: "I thought that was not a bad figure I made," he commented.

Curiously, however, this was not to be the last he would see of the mulcted traveler. The youth soon surpassed even his mother's teachings: when he was a little past sixteen years of age—he was by now dabbling in highway robbery and had hooked up with a gang of horse-thieves over the line in Mississippi—he turned his skill to opening the family treasury. He found fifty dollars; he took the money and headed north for Nashville and there, as he strolled across the Public Square, the peddler suddenly confronted him.

But the man, as it turned out, held no grudge: he was in the same game himself. His name was Harry Crenshaw; he was a stocky burly hearty fellow with a fat face and a jolly eye, and he had mixed in everything from highway robbery to murder: he had even made a voyage out from Barataria with Lafitte's pirates, and had been wrecked off the Isle of Pines. He took Murrel in hand; he had connections in the town: a few days later, the two of them were riding east on the Wilderness Road, with a drove of the gang's stolen horses, to be delivered in Georgia. They had not traveled very far before young Murrel had a chance to show his mettle.

They were coming up through the Cumberlands, and here they fell in with a young trader: he was a willing talker. "Crenshaw soon knew all about his business." His name was Woods, and he was from South Carolina. "He had been to Tennessee to buy a drove of hogs, but when he got there pork was dearer than he had calculated, and he declined purchasing." He was heading home again now, with the price of the hogs still in his pocket. That was all that Crenshaw had wanted to know.

"Crenshaw winked at me; I understood his idea." The road was skirting the edge of a ravine; there was no other traveler in sight; it was as good a time as any to get the job done. "Crenshaw asked me for my whip, which had a pound of lead in the butt. I handed it to him. . . ." The rest was almost ludicrously simple. Murrel, pointing out across the valley, uttered a sudden exclamation. Woods, gaping like a clown in a circus, turned his head to stare. And Crenshaw, reining close in on the other side, brought the butt of the whip crashing down on his skull.

He fell from the saddle. "We lit from our horses and fingered his pockets. We got $1,262." Woods was not killed, only stunned, but they had no time to finish him: at any moment some one might come spurring along the trail and surprise them. So they took the body, one by the heels and one by the head, and heaved it out over the edge of the ravine. It was a good drop down, and they watched the man go whirling to crash in the banked tree branches below. "That ought to break him up some," said Crenshaw.

They flung the saddle and bridle and all his equipment after him; they haltered his horse in with the rest of their drove and went riding on down to Georgia.

They made a long sweep westward through Alabama, heading for New Orleans; before they finished the trip two incidents occurred, both of which left a deep impression on Murrel's mind.

The first was a minor matter indeed. Coming out of Georgia Murrel had felt dizzy and chill by turns; his body ached and his eyes felt leaden; when they crossed into Alabama he could go no farther and they halted at the little town of Columbia on the Emussee River: he came down immediately with a hard fever.

He lay tossing and raving for a day or two; when he woke to his senses his body felt hollow and uncorporeal and he stuck to his bed for three days more: the innkeeper's daughter nursed him. She brewed infusions for him, brought him cup-custard to eat and noggins of milk to drink, and he lay there with his pale face on the pillow and his dark eyes staring, watching her.

He said very little, even when the time came and he rode away. Crenshaw joshed him: "Your little Miss back yonder had an eye for you, sure!" he said. "I heard her telling her pappy that you had such genteel manners as she never had seen." Murrel said nothing, but years later, at the height of his prowess along the Trace, a sudden impulse gripped him and he rode straight across the state to Columbia again, to seek out the girl and marry her. She was dead. He came back and took a girl from the "Gut," the red light district of Memphis, instead.

The second incident had an even more lasting influence on his mind. The time was about 1821, and until two years earlier Spain had hotly contested the claim of the United States to southern Alabama. The claim had finally been ceded and the state admitted in 1819 to the Union but the dispute had left disorder behind it: there was trouble everywhere.

In one community a rumor, causeless or otherwise, had spread that the negroes planned an uprising. Already, in most towns, the slaves outnumbered the whites; the fear of what might happen if the blacks ever did rebel was always worrying the settlers. At the merest hint of such a calamity, whole counties would spring to arms.

So Murrel and Crenshaw, when they entered the town, found shops shut, streets deserted, armed guards patrolling everywhere. Negroes were warned not to leave their cabins after nightfall: they would be shot on sight. Women went with a shotgun escort whenever they ventured out of doors. In the general excitement of chasing niggers nobody paid much attention to the two rovers, and they were quick to take advantage of the opportunity. They helped themselves to what funds they needed one night at the local store, waylaid a few late strollers and cleaned their pockets and rode away again in a day or two, unsuspected: everybody blamed the niggers and proceeded, no doubt, to justify their suspicions on a number of black carcasses.

The two gentlemen who had caused the disturbance rode on down to New Orleans. Crenshaw, fat and jolly, was in fine fettle, looking forward to the fun he would have in town with the girls, but Murrel all the way was thinking. He had seen the confusion that even the threat of a negro uprising could cause, and what chances for easy pickings there were for a smart man, in the hullaballoo. Suppose, then, a real rebellion could be brought about—and not one sporadic and local but planned, skilfully engineered to sweep the country—what a rich opportunity there would be for looting then! It was just an idea—a kind of dream of the bandit's heaven—but it lay in the back of his mind fermenting, until the time came when, years later, in his scheming, even dreams became plausible and he tried with an almost insane ferocity to put the project into execution.

They rode down to New Orleans: they took cover in the "Swamp," that region of shanties and shacks in the mud flats across the River, with its hive of

Such Genteel Manners

barrooms and gambling joints, and settled down for some fun. "We dressed ourselves like young lords. We frolicked for a week or more, and it was the highest larks you ever saw." It was a walloping time. They haunted the bordels: "We went to Mother Surgick's and had a real frolic with her girls. We commenced sporting and gambling, and lost every damned cent of our money."

So he woke one morning in some frowsy lady's bedroom, felt for his purse and found it empty, and set out for the road again. He still had his horse, but at Natchez he sold the animal for what he could get, bought supplies, and trudged out along the Trace. He tramped wearily for four days; he was in a bitter mood when finally, late in the afternoon, he sighted a well-mounted traveler coming spurring toward him.

As he approached, Murrel pulled his pistol and leaped in front of him. The man pulled up with a jerk and hoisted his hands; he was pale: he looked as if he were going to vomit. Murrel told him to dismount, then ordered him to walk ahead down a pebbly creek bottom that led away among the trees. Silently, hopelessly, the man obeyed.

"We went a few hundred yards until we got out of sight of the trail. Then I hitched the horse and ordered the fellow to undress. He commenced to strip, and at length stood all undressed to his shirt and drawers. Then I ordered him to turn his back to me."

And now the one terror-stricken question bubbled to the man's lips. "He asked me if I was going to shoot him: he had evidently withheld the question before. I made no answer. He stretched his hands toward me, and begged for time to pray before he died." But Murrel had no time for such whims: he told him to turn around and be done with it. So now the man knew what he must expect; his eyes widened and he looked about staring: "He looked wishfully up and down, and at last he turned from me and dropped on his knees, and I shot him through the head. I felt sorry for him, but I could not help it. I had been obliged to travel on foot for the last four days.

"As soon as he fell, I drew out my knife and ripped open his belly and took out his guts. Then I scooped up a lot of sand, stuffed it in the vacant stomach and sunk the body in the creek." So, having rid himself of the body, he set about searching the pockets of the man's clothes: "I found in all four hundred and one dollars and thirty-seven cents, and a number of papers I did not take time to look into." He did, however, have an eye to the garments themselves.

The man's coat was a rich one, and his own by now was well-worn and dusty, but he did not dare

SCENE BEFORE THE THEATRE AT NATCHEZ

"A circumstance that soon arrests the attention of the stranger is the number of **gentlemen**
with riding whips in their hands. Here all are horsemen."
——*An engraving from "Impressions of America," by Tyrone Power.*

FOR DAYTON.

THE REGULAR PATENT PACKET,

EXPERIMENT.

I. POINIER, Master.

WILL leave Cincinnati for Dayton on *MONDAY MORNING, Dec. 6, at half past eight o'clck.*

The Experiment has been lately fitted up with good accommodation for ladies. It is unnecessary to say any thing in favor of the patent improvement, as it is generally known that no packet on any canal in the U. S. can give so pleasant a conveyance. For passage apply on board or to
S. CLOON,
At the bottom of Sycamore street.

N. B. The Experiment will enter the Hamilton basin both going and returning.

N. DODGE

BEWARE OF A VILLAIN.

I WAS robbed at the tavern of John McCracken, in the town of Lexington, Ky. on the night of 30th December, 1830, by a villain who took lodgings for the night, of the sum of sixteen dollars, generously leaving me twelve & a hnlf cents, to pursue a journey of four hundred miles by stage and steam. He reported himself at Wicklift's tavern at 1 o'clock same night for Louisville via Frankfort. His name is supposed to be Ritchie. He is about common height, rather thin made, round faced, high forehead, dressed in blue broadcloth coat, drab pantaloons; when spoken to puts on a simple, mean smile, probably to prevent suspicion. He pretends to be a patent cement mender of glass, china, and crockery ware.

AARON TUFTS.

P. S. The principal constable of Frankfort, Mr. Hickman, will accept my thanks for his untiring exertion to catch the rascal, without the allurement of extra pay, and prevent him from committing further depredations on society.

The editor of the Reporter, Lexington, and Kentuckian, Frankfort, will please insert this in their papers, and forward their bills to the subscriber at Greenupsburg, Ky

January 8 53&5

A CARD.

An advertisement from the *Cincinnati Daily Gazette*, December 4, 1830, advertising one of the early steam barges; and a notice from the same journal, January 8, 1831, signalling the activities of what may well have been a member of Murrel's gang.

exchange: it might be awkward later if he were found wearing the dead man's garments. The boots, though, were another matter: "They were brand-new and a perfect fit!" And his own had never been made for hiking; after four days on the Trace they were in tatters. He kicked off the old shoes and pulled on the new ones. He swung into the saddle of his newly-acquired horse and spurred it on through the trees to the Trace again. Next day he was back in Natchez, sauntering in his glittering boots through the criss-cross of narrow alleys already known up and down the River as "Natchez-under-the-hill."

Natchez had grown from the straggling days when Mason knew it, and the Public Square where the whip had raked his back and the pillory had chafed his neck in the long penance was now a pleasant park, fresh with green grass and cool with the shade of the Pride of China trees which were spaced along its walks. The Court House—"a fine large square building surmounted by a cupola"—stood in the center of the Square; along the streets which bordered it were the stores, the business offices, the lawyers' chambers and the commission merchants' establishments—all housed in solid substantial buildings, many of which were of brick.

Natchez was rich: "The city ships more than

50,000 bales of cotton annually." Most of the planters enjoyed almost princely incomes and the beauty
of it all was that no one ever needed to hurry, no
one needed to worry: in that lush soil, under that
tropical sun the seed burst and the cotton grew
fluffy and long-fibered almost of itself; what there
was to be done the niggers could take care of, and
the gentlemen were free to loiter down Main Street
past the old tumble-down "burying ground," to doze
on the deep piazzas of Parker's Hotel, to cluster in
gossiping groups under the Grecian portico of the
Agricultural Bank, as their own spendthrift sense
of leisure inspired them. It was a time that was almost timeless, and feudal in its careless magnificence,
and the life of the town moved to the same dreamy
slow tempo.

That was Natchez above the Bluff: "under the
Hill" was another town entirely. There were two
narrow streets, and a criss-cross of narrower alley-
ways between, all spread out over the shelving mud-
flat which ran down from the base of the cliff to
the water's edge. The place was wide open, literally
and figuratively: barrooms and gambling hells overflowed into the streets; brothels had nothing more
than a curtain hung across the doorway and the girls
would lounge there, wrapped revealingly in lace
shawls or thin silk jackets, calling and beckoning

Such Genteel Manners

toward the dim room within, with its bed and its shoddy fittings, where they plied their trade.

It was a stale sordid sodden place, reeking with mud and garbage: it was heavy, too, with the more impalpable smell of sweaty lusts and savage passions.

Murder was common there. Big Jim Girty, nephew of the renegade Simon Girty, met his end at Natchez-under-the-Hill. He was a famous bully of the River: "Instead of ribs he was said to be provided with a solid body-casing on both sides, without any interstices through which a knife, dirk or bullet could penetrate." He came swaggering into Marie Dufour's saloon one night; he was spoiling for a fight and he got it. A gang of gamblers rushed him; Big Jim went down but Marie stood over him —he was her lover—with a smoking pistol and drove them off. When the fight was over and the room cleared she looked at Jim and saw that he was done for. She reloaded her pistol again and shot herself through the head.

And again: as one of the early steamers was casting off from the Landing a man sprinted out of an alley and ran up the gang-plank. He was pale, breathless; he paid his passage and started back along the boat's deck. As he did so, a rifle spoke from somewhere among the huddle of houses. The man gasped, fell, shot dead.

The Outlaw Years

The steamer's paddles were set back and she edged into the landing again; the body was put down on the shore. It lay there all day, until finally some one called the coroner. He made a brisk inspection, pronounced his verdict: "Murder against a person unknown by a person or persons unknown." The body was rolled into the river and nobody bothered any more about it.

The flimsy shanties stood so closely crowded that an outer fringe of buildings had been as if shoved bodily off the bank: they stood now with their rear ends propped on pilings, hanging swaying out over the current. Sometimes at the height of a roaring evening the rotted shoring would sag in the suck of the River: a building would cant over drunkenly; there would be a squealing, screaming stampede of the inmates before the loose-built frame structure folded in on itself and slid down bodily into the water. Sometimes the collapse would come at night, and the sleeping occupants would drift away with the building, still locked in the postures of their last drunken passions. Nobody bothered.

Natchez on the Bluff never interfered with Natchez-under-the-Hill. The sense of caste was strong, and still stronger was the frontier feeling that every man must be left to do as his own desires dictated, without interference from anybody. Whores, boatmen, gamblers, bruisers—they wanted, apparently, to live like animals and so, like animals, let them live. So long as they kept to themselves, nobody was disposed to bother them.

Sometimes a gentleman, strolling out through the pleasant park at the Bluff's top to finish a late cigar, would have his pleasure in the warm evening shattered by the uproar and brawling that went on below: "Whilst smoking my cigar here, the murmur of a fray came up to me, borne upon a light breeze. The tumult grew in loudness and fierceness; men's hoarse angry voices, mingled in hot dispute, came crashing upwards as from the depths of hell.

"I bent anxiously over the cliff"—he stared down at the crazy pattern of flaring lights and dark shadows spread out beneath him—"a louder burst ascended, then Crack! Crack! went a couple of shots, almost together:—the piercing shrieks of a female followed. . . ."

There was a silence, and then the tinny pianos, the plinking banjos in the bars took up their beat again: you could hear a girl's voice singing some bawdy song, and the men laughing drunkenly. The gentleman above on the Bluff sat down on one of the stone benches in the park and gazed out philosophically over the heavy-rolling moonlit River.

No one bothered about what went on in any of the red-light districts of the towns along the River. That such places might breed bitterer passions than any prostitute could satisfy—still more, that there the outlaws might meet and combine increasingly until no project would seem too great for them, not even the overthrow and general massacre of the upper world above them—seems hardly to have occurred to the tolerant gentlemen on the Bluff, until Murrel's conspiracy revealed it to them, just in time.

Murrel was thinking, planning, studying. He soon perceived that the old days of wanton banditry were nearly ended. Men like Mason and the Harpes could run amuck in the wilderness, and the very unpremeditated fury of their movements had saved them from capture. But nowadays travel was swifter; news got about more quickly: a lone outlaw could be tracked, hedged in, surrounded almost as soon as his identity had been discovered. The communities were in closer touch with each other than the early settlements had been: the outlaws must organize in their turn. "I soon began to see the value of friends in this business," he told Stewart. He set about making friends, and Natchez-under-the-Hill was a good place to begin.

He met a man named Carter. Carter, when he dropped down under the Hill, was as wild a roarer as any: he had a little shifty-eyed quadroon girl there, and he would sit with her and his bottle in Walton's tavern-bar, quoting Scriptures endlessly at her until some obscure instinct would drive her to fury and she would leap at him, spitting and scratching: then he would seize her and go into shouts of laughter while she stared at him, wild-eyed in his embrace.

On the road, however, Carter changed as if by magic. He traveled disguised as a Methodist preacher: he was "as slick in the tongue as goose grease." From him Murrel learned to shout sermons and sing psalms; he soon perceived how easy it would be to lay down counterfeit currency, to run off niggers and unload stolen slaves, unsuspected, in the frenzied atmosphere of the camp-meeting.

In those days, the arrival of an itinerant preacher was a magnet to draw in settlers even from the deepest wilderness. Everybody came: "I have seen from fifty to a hundred ladies, walking barefooted to the meeting, carrying their shoes and stockings in their hands"; reaching town, they would sit down by the side of the nearest "branch" or creek, wash their feet and put on their shoes. Men would come, stiff in their home-woven, home-sewn jeans. Sometimes a family would drive in with a wagon-load of produce as well, to sell for market. Hucksters put up stalls; traders and peddlers followed the evangelists as gypsies follow the fair. Saloon-keepers would move their whiskey barrels out to the edge of the field where the exhorter had taken his stand: camouflaged

in booths "composed of bushes, cut and piled up,"
they would be filling bottles for the thirsty gentlemen among the congregation.

The service itself was a frothing frenzy.[2] "I have
seen a hundred women with the 'jerks' ": they would
fall on the ground, screaming and foaming. There
would be hails of "Hallelujah! God grant it!" from
the "workers" who went stamping and clapping their
hands up and down the aisles. Men would be seen
to start forward, ripping their clothes away, staggering down to the "bull-pens" under the platform
where the reclaimed sinners rolled and slavered in
the straw. Everything went by rhythm: the "workers" with their hails, the exhorters stamping and
repeating their set phrases, the evangelist breathless
and incoherent but timing his utterance to the tom-
tom thud of a stave on the platform railing—a
rhythm that beat faster and faster, with the whole
assembly swaying in time to it, crying out in un-

[2] The "shouting revival" was introduced to the territory in the year
1802 by an itinerant preacher named Grenade: he had great success,
was called "the wild man," and left a trail of "shouting congregations"
after him. The year following, a Reverend Doak startled a revival
meeting by suddenly pitching from the pulpit and rolling all the way
down a hill in a fit of the jerks; when he came climbing back to the
stand again, he explained that "the Devil had nearly gotten him, but
God had prevailed," and went on with his sermon. Soon no sermon was
complete without a seizure; astonishing incidents occurred: once a man
who had been sitting astride a white horse, listening to the sermon, ran
amok through the crowd, spurring madly, shouting hallelujahs, until
he fell from the saddle, rigid. Several people were trampled and one
killed, but the event was hailed as a signal manifestation of divine
favor.

Such Genteel Manners

natural voices hoarse or high and squealing, frantically gesticulating, screaming, jerking, the women's very hair "popping like the crack of a whip," the men straining with gritted teeth—until in the final pitch of pandemonium sometimes even the preacher himself would catch the contagion and fall in a fit of the "jerks," pitching and tumbling down in the midst of the congregation.

After the meeting would come the let-down. Passions long pent in loneliness and now strained intolerably would give way. People would dash into the woods crying that the millennium was at hand, to be gone for days before they returned shaken and bedraggled. Others gave themselves up to long drinking bouts or fell to fighting savagely upon little or no provocation. Still others, young men and girls, fused their religious ardor with more personal impulses: "There may be some who think a camp-meeting is no place for love-making," wrote a contemporary with considerable insight. "If so they are very much mistaken. When the mind becomes bewildered and confused, the moral restraints give way and the passions are quickened and less controllable. For a mile or more around a camp-ground the woods seem alive with people; every tree or bush has its group or couple, while hundreds of others in pairs are seen prowling around in search of some cozy spot. . . ."

The Outlaw Years

With Carter for a companion, Murrel made a long circuit through the Valley: "In all that route, I only robbed eleven men, but I preached some damned fine sermons, and so scattered a lot of queer money among the pious." Carter was a "queersman"; through him Murrel got in touch with the counterfeiters at the Cave and in the dives along the River: perhaps also it was in this way that he made connection with those "influential friends," whose prestige meant so much to him.

He was traveling almost constantly. He met two gay young blades in New Orleans: Tom Phelps and Johnnie Haynes were their names. They belonged to a gang called the "Smashers"; they robbed along the Trace. Haynes was one of the "true girt" but Phelps was squeamish: he would not kill. "He has been robbing men on the highway and then letting them go on," Murrel told Stewart. "But that will never do for a robber; after I rob a man he will never give evidence against me." And true enough, misfortune overcame the fellow: he landed in jail in Vicksburg. "I fear he will hang," said Murrel, "for it would be too dangerous for us to try to get him out. . . . There is but one safe way in this business," he added, "and that is to kill. If I could not afford to kill a man I would not rob."

He worked his way up the Trace with the pair of highwaymen; they gave him a list of their friends

and confederates and then at the Tennessee Line he
left them. He rode off alone, on his own oblique and
dangerous errands. He moved here and there,
through the years that followed, watching, studying:
always his mind was twisting, coiling like a spring
tighter and tighter about that one great impalpable
idea, trying to squeeze it down to the final essence
of certainty.

The great bandit captains who had preceded him
had been the type of the true outlaw: they had
broken loose from society, plunged into the wilderness: they had, as it were, declared war on the social
order, and they fought openly. But Murrel's attack,
though no less vengeful, was more subtle. He worked
from within. He married, built a home; he cultivated friends. Instead of renouncing law and order,
he studied both. He delved in the tangled jurisprudence of the day, and out of the mix-up he evolved
that complicated argument to defeat a charge of
slave-stealing which he had been at such pains to
explain to Stewart.

He studied the naïve passionate life of the day.
Carter had shown him how easy it was to hoodwink
a man, once his religious fervor had been aroused,
and Murrel followed Carter's example. He traveled
disguised as a minister, flooding the settlements with
counterfeit; more often, he used the same disguise

in selling his stolen slaves: he found people less inclined to inquire into antecedents or to haggle over prices when dealing with a sanctimonious preacher who could say an Amen over the sale.

And slave-stealing was his principal source of income. There is no possible manner now to learn how many negroes he stole, sold over and over, and finally murdered, but that they numbered more than a hundred cannot be doubted. Murrel himself hardly knew; he remembered only those who had in one way or another struck his fancy, or whose presence had gotten him into scrapes.

There was one called Tip: "He was the liveliest devil," a frolicsome young black boy and very fond of the wenches. Murrel grew to like him; he installed him as his personal servant and took him along everywhere. But the time came, as with all the others, when Tip became too dangerous a commodity. There were too many rewards, too many descriptions of him circulating among the communities. "I felt truly sorry for him," Murrel said. "But there was no taking chances." And so the clownish Tip, pattering along with his master on some lonely highway, saw the pistol muzzle swing down to bear on his forehead, halted unbelieving, shrieked perhaps, and died.

There was another nigger named Clitto: "I got into a hell of a scrape with him." Murrel found him working in a field on a lonely plantation far down in the Choctaw country, and stopped to talk with him: "I am a great friend to the black people," he explained. Soon he had the old darky complaining about the cuffings he got from his master.

"I'll see that you get out of that!" cried Murrel. "I have carried off a great many like you, and they are all doing well, all got homes of their own and making property up North. I'll push you through."

In the end, Clitto agreed to run away that night. But Murrel perhaps had made his sales talk too strong, or Clitto was too affectionate in his nature: when he came to the rendezvous he brought his wife and three young pickaninnies with him.

This was more than Murrel had bargained for, but still he thought he could handle the situation. They struck down for the River: Murrel was making for the Arkansaw side. There was a swamp in the way, but Clitto said he knew a path through it: they all plunged in together.

The trail was a continual quagmire; finally, Murrel had to loose his horse and travel afoot, like the others. But it was messy going. At every step, their feet sank ankle-deep in the sludge, and there were always the strange, menacing swamp-sounds—the heavy bark of the alligator, the hissing withdrawal of a snake among the leaves—to trouble them. The woman tired: they piled up on a patch of high ground and slept through the rest of the night. When they woke next morning, Clitto confessed that he was lost.

Murrel was raging, but now he was tied to his victims; he was determined to get some profit out of them. He took the lead. They wandered that day and the next: "We finally killed a nest of varmints, skinned them and ate them." At last they struck an Indian trail through the bottom: it led them to the head of a bayou, and here they found a bark canoe tied along the bank.

And now the old negro chose this worst of all possible moments to rebel. Where were they going, he wanted to know: how could they be sure what kind of treatment they would get across the River? All through the famished mud-soaked journey Murrel had held his anger tamped down like a musket charge plugged in the barrel; at this faint spark of opposition it exploded.

Without a word, he whipped out his pistol, shot the negro dead. As the old man fell, the wife uttered a scream of horror. Murrel swung on her; clubbing the pistol, he smashed it savagely in her face. She dropped, dazed.. The children had scattered like chicks, and he plunged after them, kicking, pitching them headlong: when he had done with them, he returned to the mother, still sprawling; he loaded

228

his pistol, killed her. Then at last, alone, he paddled off across the River into Arkansaw.

He had already established headquarters there, near the Shawnee village in the swamps along the River. Here his men met, made their plans, and rode out again on their murderous errands. It was a hideaway when pursuit grew hot, a clearing-house for counterfeit coin, a depot where stolen goods and stolen slaves might be kept until it was safe to release them again.

And his organization was growing; its power was spreading everywhere through the territory. Murder increased: travelers rode out on the Trace and vanished. Slaves disappeared in increasing numbers: when occasionally the outraged owner tracked the thieves down and demanded his property he found his claims ignored. Witnesses turned suddenly tongue-tied in court. The sheriff, "usually a friendly man," winked while prisoners escaped. Brought to trial, an accommodating jury usually gave a verdict of acquittal. Most of the settlers robbed or defrauded, however, seldom dared go so far as to seek prosecution: they were, literally, afraid. "During the latter years of Murrel's career, the lawless elements of society undoubtedly had the upper hand of the law-abiding. The citizens lived in apprehension." So far, throughout the growth of the territory, the law had been weak and the settlers' attitude toward it disdainful. Now the time was coming when a new law was arising—that of the outlaw.

And still Murrel was riding, twisting in and out of the settlements. His genteel manners and his prideful bearing gained him acceptance everywhere. "He possessed a quick mind, and a remarkably pleasant and gentlemanlike address. He had a great natural adaptability, a certain frank, cordial manner. He was vain and eager to lead. Murrel was undoubtedly a character for whom nature had done much. . . ." He was quite willing to do something for himself, as well.

Memphis had been a boom town. At the beginning of the century, it had been the site of a military outpost and a few scattered dwellings, known so far as it might be said to have a name, by that of the hill on which it stood—the Chickasaw Bluff.

In 1819, however, a grant of the Tennessee Legislature gave 5000 acres in grant to John Ramsey and John Overton. Andrew Jackson wrote an article for the Philadelphia "Portfolio," descanting on its beauties: its streets "wide and spacious," its "ample vacant space reserved as a promenade." The place, at the time, consisted largely of vacant space but with such enticing advertisements the settlers were not slow in arriving. The boom began. Old Major Win-

Such Genteel Manners

chester the Indian fighter opened a store there. Paddy Meagher opened a tavern. Davy Crockett came along on one of his political tours, got drunk, wandered out on the Bluff to look at the River: "Hell!" he said. "I'll lay a gallon of whiskey I can jump further into that bay, make a bigger splash and wet myself less than any man here!"

"I'll take that bet, sir!" one of the gentlemen with him retorted. Crockett took one look at him: the man was a three-hundred-pounder in weight. "I give in!" he yelled; like a sportsman he paid the bet: he paid it a hundred times over. He ordered a barrel of whiskey and there, sitting out in the moonlight overlooking the rolling Mississippi, they drank it by dipperfuls. It was a wonderful party: "the biggest drunk ever known on this bluff."

Up on the Bluff it was a gay, rowdy, careless life; down among the shanties below Market Street the life was a little bitterer. This was the "Pinch-Gut," "so called perhaps because the people down there pinched their guts for whiskey": as at Natchez-under-the-Hill, it was a hive of prostitutes, a haunt of gamblers, rowdy flatboatmen. Paddy Meagher's Bell Tavern became their headquarters, and his daughter Sally was the queen of the district: "She had a head of hair and pair of eyes that would have made an ogress beautiful. She could dance the socks off any of her fair competitors in the dance."

231

The Outlaw Years

Paddy died. Sally married a dapper lad named Tom Huling, a gambler, and carried on as before. Other dives and brothels opened—Sam Stodgen's place, the Pedraza Hotel—along "Smoky Row," the main thoroughfare of the region. The people on the Bluff looked on tolerantly. Flatboatmen fought and carried on with the girls; gamblers killed each other over the gaming tables or lay in wait with knives along the gloomy alleys; it was their nature to do so and nobody bothered. Honest people had no business in the Gut anyway.

Even the town's officials left the region alone. At times there would be hundreds of flatboats ranked along the Landing, moored there waiting for the spring freshets to clear the River. Sometimes there would be a thousand or more boatmen loitering in the lower town. All these boats and all these men were supposed to be paying wharfage fees to the wharf-master, but that dignitary seldom collected. The boatmen drove him off ignominiously whenever he appeared.

"I have seen the Wharf-master streaking it up the hill, with a dozen or more fellows after him, lashing the ground at his heels with long cane poles." They would lure him out on the boats, promising to pay their fees; then they would shove off from shore and go barging downstream, to maroon the unfortunate fellow on some island and leave him

there, yelling vainly after passing boats until some
one would row out from town and rescue him.
Everybody laughed at his discomfiture—the merchants as much as the rowdies.

Sometimes, indeed, the belles of the Gut would
grow too flaunting. Moved perhaps by an obscure
impulse toward vindication, they would come tripping up the hill to edge into the life of the upper
world; they would go leering and jeering along the
Bluff where the quality promenaded.

Then the good citizens would rise in their might
and drive the intruders forth again. The town
boasted a little hand-operated fire engine: it was
called the "Vigor." They would haul the engine
out, load it full with a mixture of soap-suds and
lampblack; they would pen the painted damsels in
a corner of the promenade and flood them with the
unholy liquid until they ran, bedraggled and cursing, back where they belonged again. Everybody
laughed—the gamblers as much as the townsmen.

A definite code of mutual forbearance obtained
between the outlaws and the citizens, in Memphis
as at Natchez, Vicksburg and all the other towns.
This code had been born of the early pioneering in-
dependence; it had continued largely because the
forces of law and order were never quite strong
enough decisively to suppress the lawless. So a kind
of balance had been reached between the two factors

of society, and that balance had remained level all through the growth of the region. But now a crisis was coming: on the one hand as towns grew and trade expanded, the need for a settled government made itself felt; on the other, the same rise in prosperity and spread of traffic brought a greater number of bandits, more determined, more closely allied, to prey on it. The whole system of piracy by land and river, born in the Harpes' crazy killings and developed through Hare and Mason, was coming to its dark climax: the balance was swaying and Murrel, shrewdly calculating the weakness of the one side and the passionate bitterness of the other, was waiting, watching his chance.

He was reaching out everywhere, seeking to turn every possible circumstance to his advantage. In his dealings with the slaves, he had usually represented himself as believing that the blacks should be freed. Now, throughout the North and even occasionally in the South, a powerful anti-slavery sentiment was growing. Murrel watched its progress with great interest.

As early as 1826 Fannie Wright and Robert Dale Owens had settled in Memphis. She strode about the streets, "a tall, masculine-looking woman, with a coarse voice like a man." She organized meetings; she preached against marriage, against the Bible.

Such Genteel Manners

Suddenly she bought a plantation, stocked it with slaves: she was going to free the South.

Her idea was that each negro should be required to do only the absolute minimum of work necessary to keep the plantation in order. For any work in excess of this, he would be credited with a regular wage, until a sufficient sum had accumulated to equal his purchase price. He would then be freed and, out of the farm's profits, another slave would be bought, who in turn might work out his freedom. The settlers looked on non-committally, but Fannie was jubilant: she pictured her plantation as a sort of human mill, through which if she, or rather the negroes, worked fast enough the whole slave population of the South might be ground.

Unfortunately for the experiment, fast work was just what the negroes didn't want to do. The first batch she bought were so little excited by her notions that, far from doing excess labor, they failed even to do the required minimum. In a year or two the farm went broke, and the scheme was abandoned.

Elsewhere, however, when confronted with the opportunity of earning freedom, slaves worked manfully. Even in Memphis, Major Winchester kept a credit account open for his slaves, so that any who wished to do so might eventually work out his emancipation, and here and there throughout the South,

235

various kind-hearted slave-owners adopted similar expedients.

Others developed more fantastic plans. Hinds County, Mississippi, was the headquarters for a society whose purpose was to persuade the planters to ship their slaves bodily back to Africa, there to be incorporated in a little republic of their own: its name, appropriately, "Mississippiana." And of course, all through the North, good ladies and excellent gentlemen with powerful convictions and no very clear understanding of the facts in the case, were writing pamphlets[3] and listening to lectures designed to portray the slave-owning Southerner as nothing more or less than a cannibal, and agitating for the Government to do something about it.

How far Murrel dabbled in this mixed-up business may not be known. But that he had been in

[3] These pamphlets were of the most inflammatory description. "Lives," "Narratives," and "Adventures" of various escaped slaves—"Sojourner Truth," "Moses Grandy," "James Williams," etc.—were innumerable. One, "'A Picture of Slavery Drawn from the Decisions of the Southern Courts," affords an interesting example of how easily a series of facts individually true can be combined in a conglomerate falsehood. In this case, the author apparently went rummaging through all the southern statutes and court decisions, emerging with abundant data to prove, as the chapter-headings proclaimed, that "The Slave is Nobody—He is Like a Horse or an Ox;" "The Slave Power prevents even his Master from being Kind to Him;" "A Slave cannot avenge the Grossest Indignity Perpetrated on his Wife;" while a Georgia statute prohibiting harsh treatment of slaves, and using the words *"unnecessarily* biting or tearing with dogs," gave an excellent opportunity for the writer to dilate on the question of how much biting and tearing was considered necessary. The haze of bitterness these philippics aroused in the North still remains to cloud the true picture of slavery in the South.

communication with many of the Northern Abolitionists is certain, and it is also true that several of
his clansmen seem to have been attracted to join him
because of their convictions against slavery. Further,
he is supposed to have shown Stewart a long letter
from "a prominent Gentleman of Boston," praising
his efforts to free the slaves and suggesting that
"could the blacks effect a general concert of action
against their tyrants, and let loose the arm of destruction among them and their property, so that the
judgments of God might be visibly seen and felt, it
would reach the dirty heart of the tyrant. . . ." And
that, as a matter of fact, was just what Murrel himself was coming to believe.

He was getting closer to his idea. He was focus-
sing all his schemes, trying all sorts of large experiments. One which, at about 1829, he undertook with
Crenshaw, is interesting in its curious similarity to
that other development—the Underground Railway.
This was a plan to organize a chain of under-cover
stations stretching west to Texas, then part of the
republic of Mexico: through these stations, as along
a railway, a continuous stream of stolen slaves might
be smuggled out of the Valley and sent on for sale
in the Far West. It was a pleasant scheme: it would
permit nigger-stealing of wholesale proportions, with
no bother about pursuit afterward. So Crenshaw

was sent ahead, to arrange connections, and Murrel, having corralled a dozen or so stolen slaves, followed after.

They had no success. Some of the negroes died, some lost themselves or escaped in the wilderness; there was the constant threat of Indians all about them: it was too risky, and they never tried it again.

Murrel, however, went on down through the Spanish countries on a tour of inspection. "I wanted to see if there was no opening for a speculation in those countries. I thought I might get some strong friends there, but of all the people in the world, the Spaniards are the most treacherous and cowardly." This was certainly the opinion of an expert, at least in treachery. He was soon on the road for home again.

On his return, in 1832, the bitter blow fell. While in Nashville, he was arrested for the theft of an ornery mare (it had belonged to "a widow woman in Williamson County") ; he was tried; he was sent to jail. "The verdict and judgment was that Murrel should serve twelve months' imprisonment; be given thirty lashes on his bare back at the public whipping post; that he should sit two hours in the pillory on each of three successive days; be branded on the left thumb with the letters 'H. T.' [4] in the presence of the Court; and be rendered infamous."

The sentence was carried out to the letter. He was

[4] That is, "Horse Thief."

238

Such Genteel Manners

whipped; hooted and jeered at, he spent his period
in the pillory; on the third day he was brought in to
be branded. "At the direction of Sheriff Horton,
Murrel placed his hand on the railing around the
Judge's bench. With a piece of rope, Horton then
bound Murrel's hand to the railing. A negro brought
a tinner's stove and placed it beside the Sheriff. Horton took from the stove the branding iron, glanced
at it, found it red hot, and put it on Murrel's thumb.
The skin fried like meat. Horton held the iron on
Murrel's hand until the smoke rose two feet. Then
the iron was removed. Murrel stood the ordeal without flinching. When his hand was released, he calmly
tied a handkerchief around it and went back to the
jail."

But if he was calm without, he was not so within.
He served his year's time, and each day his anger
went deeper, his rage grew more intense. "When they
turned me loose I was prepared for anything," he
said. "I wanted to kill all but my own girt." A madness had come upon him. His mind that had been
coiled so tightly now like a released spring flew open
—and that fantastic scheme of his, for the Mystic
Confederacy and the negro rebellion, was born.

Instead of urging slaves to run away, he would
persuade them to rebel. Instead of selling them, he
would organize them: at his signal all should rise
together. His friends among the outlaws should each

have his regiment. He himself of course should be the supreme commander of them all. And when the time came, with his army of slaves behind him, with the outlaws around him, with his powerful friends paving the way before him and in every river town and wilderness crossroads a gang of skulking ruffians eagerly awaiting his coming, he would sweep in bloody and destructive fury through the country, pillaging, sacking, burning, looting—until "all but his own girt" had indeed been killed, and he himself had been raised, in omnipotent magnificence, to rule his pirate kingdom!

This was the plan of Murrel's great "conspiracy." It was a crazy scheme at best, but not so crazy then as now, and it is interesting to speculate how far he might have gone with it, had he not been betrayed. In the end of course there is no doubt that he would have failed. The towns would have risen, the honest people mobilized, the soldiers have poured in—if already his unruly troops had not wrought their own defeat by internal quarrels.

But the towns were far apart, the citizenry scattered, the Government forces far away, and before they could all have been marshaled to combat this eruption of the outlaws Murrel would have seen blood enough to satisfy even his insatiable vengefulness, in the massacres at lonely plantations, the furious encounters in swamp and wilderness that must inevitably have followed.

At any rate, once his scheme had burst upon him, Murrel gave no heed to its flaws. He was in the mood for the long chance; he had given over logic, and the outlaws in the main agreed with him. He rushed back to New Orleans: "I collected all my friends at one of our houses, and we sat in council three days, before we got our plans to our notion; we then determined to undertake the rebellion at every hazard. . . ."

He went galloping up and down the territory. He formed his Clan, with its hierarchy of officers and underlings. He mapped his ground and apportioned his districts. He sent his agents quietly proselytizing among the bewildered negroes. He organized regular meetings at a carefully chosen headquarters. He laid out his plan of battle and his lines of communications.

He had everything ready. He had a nucleus of some eighty officers and about three hundred lesser agents banded together. He had set the date—Christmas Day, 1835—and the first objective—Natchez—of the uprising. In all this, he showed no small skill as an organizer and a general—"as a soldier," a contemporary commented, "he would have had a brilliant success"—but his fate was that the same instincts of pride and vanity that had driven him in the development of his scheme were to ruin him, just short of its fulfilment.

No more grandiose conception had a more futile conclusion. He stole two niggers from an obscure parson, and a young man named Stewart rode out after him to trace the stolen property, and he told that young man everything.

DOWNFALL

MURREL AND STEWART went riding slowly on. Murrel, now that he had revealed his identity, told everything. He even told how he had decided to take the younger man into his confidence, and there is something ludicrous in the spectacle of him, hooked by his own bait and yet not knowing it, explaining fatuously: "I knew you had the true stuff in you from the first, but I wanted to test it.

"Give me an hour with a man," he said, "and I can tell you what stuff he is. I turn the talk to something shady, and if he takes the bit I give him more, until I know what he will stand. But if he seems to start back, then I make a joke of the matter and say no more. But I could see hell dance in your eyes from the minute I started talking about that elder brother. . . . It's all in knowing how to take a man," he explained patronizingly. Stewart fetched a grin, shamefaced but admiring, as of one who must admit that the joke is on him.

Murrel talked on; he mentioned at last "a matter of more importance than nigger-stealing": the Conspiracy.

The Outlaw Years

"This is a matter that is known only to a few of our leading characters," he said. "The clan are not all of the same girt."

But Stewart was to be inducted, forthwith, into the inner circle: "The first class we call the Grand Council. The second class are those we have to do what we are not willing to do ourselves. This class we call the 'strykers.' We have already about four hundred of the Grand Council and near six hundred and fifty of the strykers.

"But by the time we start off on Christmas Day, I expect we will have more than two thousand in the Clan."

He told how, all through the territory, the Clan's agents were at work, stirring up dissatisfaction among the negroes, prodding the vicious ones, inspiring them with stories of how Toussaint l'Ouverture, in the West Indies, had led blacks like themselves to freedom and glory.

How, Stewart wondered, did he take care of the danger that some simple nigger might up and give the whole show away?

Murrel assured him there was no danger there: the Clan kept them in a state of superstitious terror. "Every one that engages with us," he said, "is sworn to secrecy." And they made the matter binding in a way well calculated to impress the childlike nature of the negroes. "We have a long ceremony for the

Downfall

oath, and when we give it we show them a monstrous picture of a great devil, to teach them obedience, and the skeleton of a man, to show them what will happen if they are unfaithful. . . ."

Murrel's friendship was overwhelming: like some wild beast grown suddenly fawning, he seemed only the more dangerous for his flattering advances. "I'll make a man of you," he said.

"By God!" he said. "I'll show you the plumpest girls that ever come across!"

He would make the lad his personal aide. "Hues," he said, "I want you to be with me at New Orleans the night that the niggers commence their work!"

He explained how the rebellion was to begin simultaneously in several places; then close in on itself, gathering strength as it were centripetally; then sweep triumphantly down the River.

His bitterness had sunk deep: all his hopes now were focussed on the destruction of others: "I intend to head the company that attacks New Orleans. I have always wanted to smash that city. Think of it, Hues—even the British couldn't take it!"

He was reminded of a curious incident that had occurred in his earlier days, when he robbed along the Trace. He had been jogging northward toward the Tennessee country, when a very paragon of elegance came spurring behind him. "I was overtaken by a tall and good-looking young man, riding an elegant horse, and the young gentleman's whole get-out was the richest that could be had." They saluted each other, as travelers will; they fell to talking.

"We rode on, and soon got very intimate, and agreed to be company through the Choctaw Nation." Murrel himself was a prideful dresser: each admired the other's outfit. "We were two damned fine-looking men, and to hear us talk we were very rich.

"I felt him on the subject of speculation, but damn it, he cursed the speculators, and said he was in a bad condition to fall into the hands of such damned villains, as he had the cash with him that twenty niggers had sold for." At this, Murrel needed no further encouragement.

It was a lonely country. The tall young man rode on, loose in his saddle, gesturing, boasting; Murrel waited his chance.

They came to a place where the Trace crossed the dry bed of a creek. Murrel said he was very thirsty; he said that, up the creek a ways, there was an excellent spring. They drew up, their horses prancing. "You first, sir," said Murrel courteously, and the proud young gentleman went clattering ahead up the gully. Murrel followed, until they were out of sight of the trail.

"I drew my pistol and shot him through. He fell,

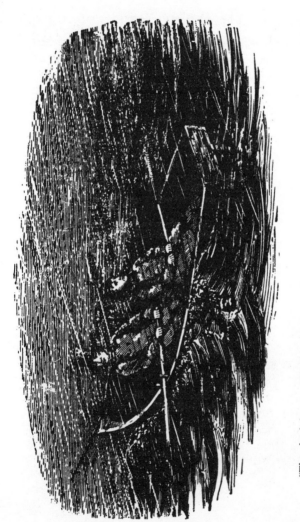

"They landed at a point opposite the mouth of the Old River, which joins the Mississippi at the Chickasaw Bend."
—A print from "The Life and Adventures of John A. Murrell."

"Many planters made as much as twenty thousand dollars a year."
—*An engraving from "Das Illustrierte Mississippithal."*

dead." And that was where the joke came in. "Well, sir, I commenced hunting for his cash. I found a large pocketbook and it was stuffed full; when I began to open it I thought it was a treasure indeed.

"But Oh! The contents of that book! It was filled with copies of songs, and forms of love letters, and clippings of poems and some of his own writing—but no cash.

"I began to cut off his clothes with my knife, and examine them for his money. . . . I found four dollars and a half in change, and no more! Well, thought I, and is this the amount that twenty niggers was sold for?" The joke had been on himself, and Murrel laughed, but a little bitterly: "The damned young hypocrite. But it served him out as he deserved!"

They rode all day, and that night they stopped at a small inn that lay just back from the Mississippi River; the inn was kept by a man named Jonathan Champeon. This was to be their last day on the Tennessee side.

For three days Stewart had been riding, gaping, nodding, admiring, listening to this man's tales of lust and blood and murder. "He had heard him recount the black deeds of his life until his blood had frequently chilled. He was not willing for Murrel to escape justice any longer": and yet at the thought of what lay before him his blood grew colder still, with fear.

For next day, they would cross into Arkansaw. Next day they would be in the Clan's headquarters. So far, after all, he had had but one man to outwit, one man to face if it came to fighting, but over there he would have not one but dozens of enemies to contend with, and on their own ground, in their own headquarters. He knew that once he crossed the River he would be abandoning all hope of resistance or escape; he knew that if by the merest chance or error he were betrayed it would mean his certain end, and worse, no word of his ending would ever, perhaps, be heard. Crossing the River, the young man felt, would be like crossing into death itself and like even the most disheartened suicide he wanted to leave some message to explain his going. He could not bear to face, without a word, such total oblivion.

They were the only lodgers at the little inn; that evening they sat in the common room with the landlord, talking by the fireplace. The landlord was a lank quiet fellow, imperturbable and slow; he listened a great deal and said very little: he resisted Murrel's best efforts to draw him out. Stewart watched him; the man seemed honest. But honest or not, Stewart felt he must tell somebody, or break down completely.

And so next morning when Murrel and he had

traveled some little distance from the inn, he muttered something about a pair of gloves and came rushing back to Champeon again.

He must have made a bewildering figure, starting in on the tavern-keeper, glancing back over his shoulder and then blurting out his incoherent tale of nigger-stealing, conspiracy and murder. He hurried his words: he was almost babbling. No, there was nothing he wanted; nobody could help him; he had to go on, alone. Only, if he didn't come back, he wanted to ask that some word of his going would be sent on to Parson Henning. Champeon, in his slow way, promised that the message would be delivered.

And again, Stewart asked, could the other spare him a pistol? He would feel safer. Champeon gave him a pistol.

And then Stewart darted away again, hurrying to rejoin the waiting Murrel.

Murrel, when he got back, was grumbling: "You took a long time about a damned pair of gloves!" he said.

They got down to the River, and there their troubles began. It was high water: the flood had swept in through the low lands along the bank, blocking the trail to the bayou where the Clan's private ferry was hidden. So they pushed on up through the bottoms, slipping and sliding sometimes where the swamp-mud had frozen, sometimes plunging knee-deep in the icy water when the crust broke beneath their weight.

At last they emerged at a tiny clearing and cabin, owned by a Parson Hargus. He had a boat, an old skiff, but so rotten and leaky that it seemed it would hardly carry them. But the rage that always flamed in Murrel when an obstacle blocked him was blazing now: he would take that boat and cross in it, or sink.

They set out, rowing furiously, but the rip of the current caught them and swept them into the bend. They made back for the shore again; they landed three miles lower down, at a Mr. Irvin's plantation.

They rested there. Murrel did a bit of business: he said he was a negro-trader; after his errand across the River had been accomplished he was going back into Tennessee to fetch a bunch of slaves for sale down the River. Irvin spoke for three field hands, and Murrel agreed to deliver them in two weeks' time.

Then they set out again in the skiff, and this time they made the crossing. They landed just opposite the mouth of the Old River, in the break of the Chickasaw Bend.

Here there was nothing but swamp and desolation, a long flat rain-stricken freezing stretch of cane-brake and swamp-willows. Murrel led the way, striking out along a trail that only he could trace; Stewart, following through the dim trees and the misty silence, felt himself already half a ghost.

They came to a lake, and a hut on its bank. There were a couple of men lounging in the doorway, and a couple more at a table inside, drinking. There were four negroes sitting quietly, backs to the wall, in a corner of the room. The men were wild-looking fellows, heavily armed. They saluted Murrel; then one led the way down to a landing and ferried them over the lake. And then Murrel and Stewart plunged into the swamp again, slogging through the mud, climbing over rotted logs. . . .

Murrel put his hand to the other's arm and halted him. "Do you see yonder cottonwood that rises above the other trees?"

"Yes. I see it."

Murrel gave his arm a little intimate exultant shake. "That stands in the Garden of Eden. That is headquarters!"

The clan's headquarters was a large low building of fresh-cut logs, built like an Indian council-house, with one long room and a number of smaller chambers opening, alcove fashion, along the side. The place was sparse of furniture: there were bear hides and piled straw-bedding in the alcoves; in the large room, save for a few chairs and a long trestle table, the furnishings consisted mostly of what the previous passing tenants had left behind. There were old shirts, worn boots, empty bottles, a ripped pair of breeches, shoved aside here and there in the vacant corners; a rusted knife, bits of shattered crockery lying half-embedded in the earthen floor.

Pegs had been driven between the logs in the wall, and here were hung the belongings of the present occupants, their saddle bags and holsters, shot-pouches, leather shirts. All the old smells that each article harbored the rain and the swamp-damp had revived again: the place reeked of sweat, stale whiskey, leather and manure.

Some ten or eleven men were grouped about the fireplace where a huge log was burning; Murrel made for it, for a dry and a warm. The others made way for Stewart and saluted the chief; later, a dozen more men drifted in, as the news spread that Murrel had arrived.

There were greetings and questionings. Why weren't there more men on hand, Murrel wanted to know. They told him, many had been held at their homes by the hard season and the cold; several who had come had waited a day or two and then gone off again, thinking Murrel himself had decided not to come: "They had got uneasy about him."

Downfall

Murrel fell to cursing, explaining how the high water and the rain and the difficult crossing had held him up. He had had a hell of a time and he blamed it all on that "fool Henning: the damned old preacher's niggers had cost him more trouble than any he had ever stolen in all his life." Stewart, who had almost forgotten that he had started out originally to trace his friend's slaves, pricked up his ears.

Where, Murrel demanded, were the niggers? A man named Lloyd spoke up: in the chief's absence he had taken charge. He said that "the niggers had come in badly frost-bit, and so they thought it best to push them as soon as possible. They had sent the two niggers and three others and seven horses down the River on a trading boat, to the Yazoo market. And they had given the men in charge several thousand dollars in counterfeit, to sell along the way."

There was drinking. Stewart was introduced, and made a member of the Clan. "They gave him the two degrees in signs, which belong to the two classes. He first received the sign of the stryker": this was a wave of the hand, with the wrist bent in a peculiar fashion. "Then they gave him the sign of the Grand Counsellor": a hand-shake with the fingers closed against the palm.

It was a childish business, no doubt, but one in which the minds of those primitive ruffians delighted.

The Outlaw Years

They hailed the new member and shook hands with him by turns. "He was practised by them until he could give and receive the signs as well as any."

More whiskey was drunk. Everybody was fuming up for a real stamping thrashing smashing drunk; they pressed Stewart to drink, but he dared not. There is a moment when antipathy must show itself —if not in words at least in the look, or the gesture, or the single freezing instant when the only possible expression is disgust—and he felt that moment was rapidly approaching. Drunk, he would be sure to betray himself; even, sober, he could hardly contain himself.

It began to seem almost as if they were egging him on. Murrel was blustering, boasting: what wouldn't he do to old man Henning, some day! By God! He would give five hundred dollars to have him over into Arkansaw, and he went on to say how he would torture him. But as far as that went, let him stay in Tennessee; they would haul him out of his bed some fine night and give him his dressing down: two hundred lashes on his bare back might teach him to mind his business. Stewart listened with a frozen grin.

And at last he felt he had to get away. He called Murrel aside; he told him he was going. "I'll wait across the River for you, at Irvin's."

Downfall

Murrel, half drunk and riotous, laughed at him. "You don't want to go now. Fun's just beginning!" Anyway, there were plans to be discussed to-morrow: stay till to-morrow.

Stewart said he would leave his vote in Murrel's hands and Murrel, flattered; nodded. Weaving, he tried to find another argument: "Look here! To-morrow we'll get in a load of Arkansaw girls and have a regular frolic!"

Stewart said there was a girl at Irvin's he wanted to see. At this, Murrel grinned and winked and poked him jovially. So that was it! Well, then. . . .

Stewart, with a relieved heart—"he breathed easy, he felt, for the first time in four days"—ferried back across the River. He stayed that night at Irvin's; he told the man his story, and arranged with him to have a guard concealed about the house when Murrel came back from Tennessee with his slaves. In this way, they could catch him with the goods.

And next day, when Murrel came across the River, the two rode out again, toward Madison County and home.

They rode as far as Wesley together, and here they parted, for Stewart pretended that he was bound down south for the Yalo Busha. As he left, Murrel wrote out for him a long list of nearly one hundred

255

names—all clansmen he might meet along the way. Stewart started south; in a mile or two he doubled east, to cut in ahead of Murrel on the road to Madison.

And three days later, when Murrel rode in at his plantation, a dozen armed men were waiting for him. Murrel took the matter with the utmost confidence: he had been arrested before.

They questioned him. Where had he been?—Over into Arkansaw on a business trip. Alone?—No, a young fellow named Hues had ridden with him most of the way. A friend of his?—Hardly, he had met the fellow for the first time in his life at Estanaula.

And then the farmers sprang their surprise. "Mr. Hues," the sheriff called, and Murrel saw his young friend pushing forward from the crowd. At the sight, Murrel's nerve almost broke: "Murrel for the first time lost his spirits and fortitude. He appeared as though he would faint, and they gave him water several times before he recovered."

But later, as he was being transported under heavy guard to the county jail at Jackson, he recovered his bravado. "Who is that fellow Hues? Does he live around here?" he asked.

The officer, who had been told to keep Stewart's identity secret, replied non-committally: Hues was a stranger in those parts; he didn't know much about him.

Downfall

"Well," said Murrel, "he had better remain a stranger. I have friends."

It was a strange situation. Stewart had planned to capture Murrel at Irvin's, when he might be taken with stolen slaves actually in his possession. But the long-thwarted farmers at Madison had overruled him, and now the only evidence against Murrel was the testimony of Stewart himself. They set out to find some corroboration for that.

A sheriff's posse rode down with Stewart to the River, and crossed into Arkansaw; they searched the swamp from end to end, and they found nothing but the abandoned camp and the hut on the lake: word had passed ahead of them, through the Clan's mysterious channels, and all the men they sought had flown.

They rode down the River, hunting the boatload of slaves that had been bound for the Yazoo Market. That, too, had disappeared.

They posted a guard at Irvin's, on the chance that some other agent might come in to sell the slaves. No one turned up.

Murrel lay quietly in jail, chatting with his guards; his wife visited him daily. He seemed so docile that at last the guards grew careless, and one night—with saws smuggled in by his wife, with a horse waiting outside supplied by an unsuspected townsman—he broke jail and vanished.

But the sheriff's men rode hot on his trail, and an easy trail it was to follow, for it was strewn with articles known to belong to Murrel—a hat, a pistol, a writing pad, an overcoat—and they galloped heartily along until the trail led them into a swamp and ended there with a mocking suddenness. Murrel had planned his escape so well as to have arranged beforehand that one of the Clansmen should lay down this false scent for the pursuers. He himself had been smuggled out of the State and into Alabama, concealed in a wagon-load of grain.

But they caught him; he was recognized in a tavern near the Muscle Shoals, on the old military road to Fort Deposit. They brought him back to Jackson and there, like a wildcat raging against the bars, he was jailed again. Trial was set for July.

Murrel was not the only man to worry about the situation: he had sent word to the Clansmen confessing that he had given Stewart a list containing many of their names, and now these accomplices saw sudden ruin staring at them: "Many of them had stood fair in society, and they were desperately pestered for what would happen." So far, Stewart had not revealed his list, he had hardly more than hinted at the existence of the Conspiracy: he was saving all that for the trial, and all up and down the Valley shady bankers, slippery traders and cozening merchants and smart men generally who hadn't objected to mixing a dishonest penny or two with their honest ones, were scrambling and sweating for some way to forestall the disclosure.

And the way, after all, was clear. "There were but two alternatives: they must either destroy the character of Stewart, or he would destroy them." Stewart was the sole witness; they must, obviously, destroy his claim to credibility.

And so, all through the territory, vague and ugly rumors began to circulate. Stewart's father had been a horse thief in Georgia and the son was no better. People down in the Choctaw Purchase had left off trading at his store: everything he dealt in was shoddy; his partner had left him, swearing he was a robber. He had been ducked in mud and caned off a river boat, for cheating at cards. He was wanted in Alabama, as a counterfeiter.

In all this, Murrel's boasted legal knowledge stood him in good part. He occupied his time in jail in drawing up a sort of circular letter, which he sent out through his lawyers, ostensibly to aid in accumulating evidence for his defense. Actually, it was designed to destroy the value of Stewart's testimony, first by attacking his character and, more directly, by

259

proving that he had a personal interest and profit to be derived by obtaining Murrel's arrest.

The letter was in the form of a certificate:

"This day personally appeared before us, etc., Jehu Barney, James Tucker, Thomas Dark, Joseph Dark, Wm. Loyd, etc., etc., who, being sworn in due form of law, do depose and say that they were present and saw . . . Steward of Yellow Busha, in the evening of the first day of February last, in company with John Murrel, at the house of said Jehu Barney, over the Mississippi River; and that he the said Steward informed us that he was in pursuit of John Murrel for stealing two negro men from Preacher Henning, in Madison County near Denmark; and that he had told Murrel his names was Hues, and he wished us to call him Hues in Murrel's hearing. We also recollect to have heard him, the said Steward, say distinctly that he was to get five hundred dollars ($500) for finding the said negroes and causing said Murrel to be convicted for stealing them. Said Steward did not say who was to give him this reward, but he stated that he held the obligation of several rich men for that amount.

Signed................"

Lloyd, Barney, Dark and the rest had been chosen because, aside from their association with the Clan, they were occupied as merchants, wood-traders, etc., in the Arkansaw country, and lived on the outskirts of the swamp where the Clan had met.

Consequently, if Stewart admitted having confided in Irvin and Champeon on the east bank of the River, it might be adduced that he had confided in others, ostensibly as honest, on the farther bank. According to this representation, the Clan's headquarters became nothing more than a sort of winter camp in the swamp, where a group of honest toilers of the neighborhood met to disport themselves, and into which Stewart, under an assumed name, had intruded himself, while his supposed admission that he was to get five hundred dollars reward for the arrest gave ground for the assertion that he had invented all the evidence on which Murrel had been arrested, purely to collect the money.

At the same time, Murrel inclosed an explanatory letter, with his circular, touching on Stewart's character by a clever innuendo which was given added force by his manner of mentioning the matter in an aside, as if of something too well known to need insisting:

"The above is a copy given to me, by one who heard him make the admission therein contained in your presence. You will therefor please send me the names of all that will testify to these facts in writing, and also send me the names of all and every man that will certify these witnesses to be men of truth.

J. MURREL

"P. S. But above all things, arrest him for passing the six twenty dollar bills. You will have to go out into the Yellow Busha County, near the centre, for him. Undoubtedly this matter will be worthy your attention, for if it be one, two, or three hundred dollars, the gentleman to whom he passed it, can present it before a Magistrate and take a judgment for the amount, and his provision store, etc., is worth that much money.

"My distressed wife will probably call on you, and if she does, you may answer all her requests without reserve.

Yours, etc., etc.,

J. MURREL."

So, in growing venom, matters moved on into Spring. Stewart had been chased out of Kentucky with the irate father of a girl he had ruined at his heels. Another man had it on good authority that the reason Stewart had left Yalo Busha was because the man at whose house he boarded had objected to Stewart's attentions to his wife.

Stewart had always been a wanderer; he was a young fellow, completely alone: against such rumors, issuing from sources of such impregnable respecta-

Downfall

bility, he was more or less powerless. People who had been his friends now avoided him. It began to look as if not Murrel, but Stewart himself, were on trial.

Almost the only place he had ever struck foot down and settled was at Yalo Busha, and so now, in his dismay and consternation, he decided to return there, until the trial. He would go back to the Vess family, who had always had a pot boiling with coffee on the stove for him; to Clanton, who had helped him so kindly with his affairs.

His return was a fresh disillusionment.

Vess met him at the cabin; he "looked very wild and confused." Mrs. Vess gave him a heartier greeting—almost, again, too hearty—but there was a straining tension in the air: they watched him furtively. Like a sudden flood of dirty water spurting up through a thousand crevices, the hidden currents of the underworld had inundated the territory; in Tennessee it had almost sucked him under and now he saw the tide had carried even here: here it had swamped the foundations of his life. For the first time, he began to feel actually afraid.

How much he had to fear he was soon to discover. He had arrived late; Vess and his wife had finished their meal but Mrs. Vess insisted on fixing up a snack for him. He refused—in his discouragement he had no appetite for food—but she pouted and insisted. At least, he would have a cup of coffee, like he always used to: a cup of coffee and a piece of hoe-cake, after his travels.

She flounced out into the kitchen lean-to, and came back after a time with a hot cup steaming. He stared at it: he could not touch it. And suddenly, all the coaxing faded from her face, and it was hard and bitter with some unreadable emotion. Stewart got up wearily and went out into the dooryard. "He walked out and got under a cart bed which was leaning against the house": standing there unobserved and at first unobserving, he saw what went on within the house.

The cat jumped up on the table; it prowled over to the cup he had left there, stuck out a tentative tongue. Mrs. Vess saw it; she whirled, cried out, and snatched the animal away. Vess made some grumbling comment. His wife replied, "Never mind. It's my cat!" And then, with great care, she took up the coffee cup, carried it out to the rear door, and poured the contents on the ground.

It was all so odd that at first it seemed incomprehensible to the stunned Stewart. And then, in a flash, he understood. The cup had been poisoned! They had meant to poison him!

A few days later, he had a strange confirmation of all his suspicions. He had moved, with all his be-

Downfall

longings, to the cabin of an old bachelor named
Sanders. But he was restless: he spent a good deal of
his time wandering out beyond the town in the surrounding forest, pondering the strange situation into
which he had been projected.

And as he walked, one day, a stranger came riding: a man with a big bulldozing bearded face and
a holster of pistols swung from the saddle before him.
A picture of the desperado, as he came booting his
jaded horse along. When he came abreast of Stewart
he hailed him.

He asked directions to the town, and Stewart told
him. And finally the great bulky fellow blurted out
the question, "Do you know of a man named Virgil
Stewart, living there?"

Stewart, suspecting everybody, had already been
wondering what the man's errand might be, and now
he was sure of it. He calculated his answer to seem
a little cold. Yes, he said, but as if the subject dis-
pleased him, he knew Stewart.

The rider seemed surprised at the tone. "What!
Don't you like him, sir?"

"I have seen people I like as well."

The man settled himself crosswise in the saddle
and stared, then grinned slyly. "And why don't you
like him, if I may inquire?".

"Why," said Stewart, still affecting a certain reserve. "It seems to me that he interferes too much in things that don't concern him."

And now, cautiously, the rider gave the sign of the Clan. Stewart answered it, and the man let loose with a burst of loutish satisfaction. "Oho!" he cried. "So you are up to it, eh?"

Stewart was up to it, and the fellow, with almost childish pleasure, dismounted awkwardly to chat with his new friend. His name, he said, was George Aker. "I am sent on by the Council to stop the wind of that damned Stewart, and I want you to help me." With all his bluster, murder seemed not to be an errand he liked to tackle alone.

Stewart told him just enough to make him tell more—that his name was Tom Goodin, that he himself had been after Stewart, but waiting his chance for a sure kill—and soon Aker was revealing everything.

He told how Vess had been given one hundred dollars to poison Stewart, and how that had failed. He told how Clanton as well was a power in the Clan: "The fellow with whom he works is a good friend to us." Clanton had promised to make charges that Stewart had embezzled funds from the store, and had passed counterfeit money in the town, but he had some compunctions still: "Clanton has always been friends with him," said Aker, and he told how

Downfall

Clanton's friendship had taken a curious paradoxical turn. "He will make no charges against Stewart while he is living, do you see, but directly he is killed, Clanton will come out with it."

Vess, too, would charge adultery against his wife. Others were ready to appear, swearing that Stewart had dealt out counterfeit money to them. It only remained, then, to get Stewart killed: to accomplish this he, George Aker, had been sent; he was to be paid two hundred dollars if he succeeded.

If he failed, then the Clan's last resort would be to send a posse of subsidized officers of the law from Arkansaw, to extradite him thither on a charge of counterfeiting. And Aker grinned: "When we get him back over the Mississippi, we will give him hell; we will give him something to do besides acting the spy; we will speechify him!"

The conversation ended in an extraordinary proposal: Aker offered to split his two hundred dollars with Stewart, if he killed that sneaking hypocrite, Stewart! And Stewart gravely agreed. He urged Aker to camp out of town that night, in order not to put Stewart on his guard by the arrival of a stranger; and they parted, Stewart agreeing to meet him again next day, with the news that Stewart was dead.

Stewart never saw the man again: discreetly inquiring, he learned enough to conclude that the blundering fellow had learned of his error, and had

267

decamped. But thenceforward, until the day of the trial, Stewart slept with a barred window, and never moved without a brace of pistols ready.

The trial was held at Jackson, at the sessions of the Circuit Court, in July, 1834. Murrel came well defended; his chief counsel was no less a personage than the Honorable Milton Brown, Esq., who was ten years later to attain worthier fame by introducing in Congress the bill by which Texas was annexed to the United States. In the present instance, he was chiefly distinguished for the savagery with which he attacked the testimony of Stewart.

The whole matter, as had been foreseen, had boiled down to the question as to whether or not Stewart's story could be believed. He was the State's only important witness; he stood in the little railed-off docket before the judges' seat and read out, painstakingly and conscientiously, the entire transcript he had made of the conversations with Murrel on that famous ride.

It took hours; it occupied a whole afternoon and morning of the court's proceedings but he read every word. There were loud guffaws and consequent poundings of the judges' gavel when he read off, portentously, Murrel's remarks on the girls in Arkansaw. There were heavy silences, mixed of incredulity and amazement, when the Conspiracy was mentioned, and all the ramifications of Murrel's organization appeared. There was almost a riot, when Murrel's list of Clansmen was read and partisans and enemies of the men named hooted or cheered.

When Stewart stepped down, the State's case, save for a number of character witnesses to vouch for his honesty, was at an end. It was noon of the second day, and the Court adjourned for dinner. In the afternoon, the defense had its turn.

Murrel had planned to call to his aid an imposing array of his friends but these, as the matter progressed, had one by one deserted him: all the smart men who had been hand-in-glove with him were withdrawing the hand, and the glove was left very limp indeed.

Brown, however, had discovered a point that he rather fancied, in the fact that Stewart admitted having taken the Clan's oath and accepted its sign-ritual, only to betray it. With this for entering wedge, he hammered home a bitter and relentless attack on Stewart himself. He was noted for his sharp wit and his acid phrases, and to-day he surpassed himself.

He dragged out all the scandalous rumors that had been circulated and paraded them; he spoke of Cain and Abel; he maintained that an oath, however taken, was forever binding, and the man who broke it was a sneak and a knave. He roared and thundered, but it was all empty shouting and everybody—except possibly Stewart who sat in a pale tense heat of resentment through the long jeremiad—knew as much.

At the end of the afternoon, Milton Brown waved his hand, wiped his high portentous brow that was now glistening with sweat, and sat down.

Half an hour later, John A. Murrel, found guilty of negro-stealing and of selling stolen negroes, was commanded by the Court to rise and hear his sentence.

He rose obediently, and stood with his head lowered and his face beet-red with the last great rage that burned within him. He was sentenced to serve a period of ten years, at hard labor, in the State Penitentiary at Nashville. Then he sat down, as if automatically; he sat wooden and motionless, until the sheriff and his guards came and seized his arms and led him away. A great crowd, hostile and jeering, followed him across the Court House Square to the door of the county jail.

A few days later, he was sent on to Nashville, under heavy guard. There, among others who came to look at the noted bandit, was the learned Professor O. S. Fowler, phrenologist of wide repute. By special arrangement with the authorities, he was permitted to read the bumps on Murrel's head.

He found, as might have been expected, that "Energy, Acquisitiveness were fully developed; Secretiveness, quite large; Self-Esteem, large and active;

Downfall

Adhesiveness, slight. . . ." In sum, the Professor stated: "He has natural Ability, if it had been rightly called out and directed, for a superior Scholar, scientific man, lawyer or a Statesman."

THE FOURTH OF JULY

MURREL was in jail, ruined, betrayed. His wife, with her household, moved out of the territory; his strange friends vanished mysteriously, retreating again to their hiding places in swamp and wilderness. Lawyer Brown, strolling debonairly on the streets of Nashville, was suddenly confronted by Stewart, horsewhip in hand and determined to avenge the other's insults at the trial: only the intervention of bystanders saved Murrel's advocate from a thorough thrashing. Lawyer Brown left town next morning.

Stewart, still fearing for his life, set out a few days later for Lexington, Kentucky. Passing Patton's Ferry, a few miles out from Nashville, he was waylaid by three ruffians. He spurred against them, firing his pistol; his quick action disconcerted their aim but one of them, making a bludgeon of his rifle, caught the young man a clip on the shoulders that "was like to have unjointed his neck."

He got away; he rode, dizzy with pain, clinging to the saddle-horn, until he had outdistanced their pursuit. Then he fell over in a field and lay there, half delirious, until dark; by night, he continued his journey.

272

The Fourth of July

Reaching Lexington, he found the security he craved. The Clan could not reach him there and so, in tranquillity, he drew up a digest of his testimony at the trial: he included his description of the famous trip into Arkansaw, his conversations with the bandit, his experiences at the Clan's headquarters, and the complete list of fellow-conspirators which Murrel had given him. The whole document was published in pamphlet form and distributed through the territory; almost immediately, a series of self-constituted commentators rewrote the material in narratives each a little more blood-curdling than the last, until finally the astute editor of the Police Gazette capped them all with a penny-dreadful "pictorial Life" of the "GREAT WESTERN LAND PIRATE."

Stewart had intended his pamphlet as a vindication and a warning: in both respects, it failed. Murrel was in jail and thus, obviously, harmless. At times before the trial—in the ease with which the bandit had escaped, the almost magical way in which all evidence against him vanished out of the path of the searching posses—men had sensed uneasily that there were dark forces massing behind the bandit leader, but all that had faded now. And as for all this talk of conspiracy and rebellion, nobody, frankly, believed it.

The Outlaw Years

It was too mad a scheme for a normal mind to credit and what little disposition there was to believe in it was doused in the ridicule and baffled by the vilification to which Stewart himself had been subjected. Those random tales of counterfeiting, wife-stealing, embezzling had had their bite and now Stewart, crying his fantastic warning through the wilderness, met with nothing but laughter and disbelief.

It is characteristic of the situation that at the conclusion of the pamphlet he felt it necessary to include a series of sworn statements by his various friends and business associates, attesting to his honesty and trustworthiness. And it is characteristic of the essentially sporting attitude generally prevailing toward the law and toward ethics at the time, that all this testimony had little weight against the widespread feeling that it was a pretty rotten trick for one man to listen to another man's secrets and then betray them. The hardy westerners had no use for Stewart's brand of amateur sleuthing.

The Clan, however, continued. Headless now, it moved on fumblingly; as some swamp-reptile might twitch and thresh about, blind but dangerous still, long after its brain center had been destroyed, so the Conspiracy survived as if by instinct in the vague plottings of swamp-refugees, in a formless restless resentment among the rowdy denizens of the river towns.

Here and there—on an island in mid-Mississippi, at a lonely camp in the canebrake in the Choctaw Purchase—little groups of Clansmen met and argued and strove blunderingly to formulate their plans. Their one shrewd move was to change the date that had been set for the uprising: instead of waiting until Christmas and thus giving the authorities time to prepare for them, they decided to forestall resistance by signaling the rebellion for the Fourth of July.

And so, through the year that followed Murrel's trial, the pot that he had set boiling continued to simmer and stew. It was a time of bitterness and resentment: the old democracy of the pioneers was splitting up into castes and classes, each a mark for the animosity of the others. Riverman hated landsman, the flatboatman hated the steamboat crew, the poor man hated the arrogant rich and the outlaw hated them all.

Murrel had been shrewd enough to sense this conflict of interests in the social order and capitalize it; lacking his direction, however, the Conspiracy lost itself in the very criss-cross of passions it sought to control. When at last the fuse was laid and the match applied, the whole rebellion spent itself in a series of scattering and sporadic explosions of petty hatred and localized animosity: it is likely that, in all the crowds that rioted and blustered through the river-towns, not one participant in ten had any idea of what the fighting had been, originally, about.

All they knew was that, for months, there had been bitterness and evil feeling; for months, men's passions had been strung tighter and tighter until at last they jangled loose in impatient and unconsidered action. Men struck out pointlessly; they made strange gestures, menacing but ineffectual.

In Vicksburg, a gambler named Cabler suddenly appeared, drunk and boisterous, at the field outside town where the Vicksburg Volunteer Rifle Corps was holding its annual muster and barbecue. He insisted on having a seat at table; he swore he was as good as any one there. He plunged about, jostling, jeering, mouthing obscenities: he was obviously bent on getting into trouble. One of the officers of the company remonstrated with him. Cabler immediately struck him down.

Others leaped forward. In a twinkling the shady grove with its long tables set out around the roasting pit, its little groups of preening gentlemen and ladies decorously smiling, was in disorder. The ladies screamed and scurried; men milled about, overturning tables, driving toward the spot where the clash had begun.

Cabler found himself suddenly hedged about with flailing arms and furious faces. He drew his pistol, but now that the trouble had started he seemed himself a little bewildered. He stood a moment, vaguely waving the weapon; suddenly he whirled and ran back through the town again: people saw him, still with his pistol drawn, go galloping insanely down the quiet streets, to disappear among the tumbled shanties at the Landing.

But later as with glittering arms and gleaming uniforms the Vicksburg Volunteers paraded in the Public Square a frightened negro pot-boy from one of the river-side taverns came running with a formal message from the gambler, notifying all and sundry that he was coming back again, "armed, and resolved to kill."

He appeared. The impeccable Volunteers charged bayonets. Cabler never had a chance: he was arrested, disarmed. "A loaded pistol and a large knife and dagger were found." Indignant citizens trussed him—and then a peculiar problem presented itself: on what possible charge could he be held? "The Law could not reach him, since he had not committed the crime intended; to free him would insure his vengeance. . . ." What could be done with the annoying fellow?

277

"It was determined to Lynch him, which is a punishment provided for such as become obnoxious in a way the Law cannot reach." So Cabler faced his inglorious martyrdom; all his bitter rage had vanished: he waited numbly while the mob pressed about him.

"He was carried out under a guard, attended by a crowd of respectable citizens"; they brought him to the very grove where the barbecue had been held. They halted near the roasting pit, still smoking from the feast, and here another council was held and a gentler punishment decided on. "He was tied to a tree, punished with stripes, tarred and feathered, and ordered to leave the city in 48 hours."

But that night, a sortie was made from the red-light district by the gambler's friends. It was as ineffectual as Cabler's crazy gesture had been. They blustered up and down the streets; like bats, they went swooping and blundering: at last, having accomplished nothing, they went straggling back to their own dark dens again.

So it was with the other towns. Natchez-under-the-Hill was the scene of a bloody battle between the flatboatmen and the roughs of the gambling dens. Everywhere the blind mob-impulse ruled.

In Memphis, good citizens enjoying the afternoon promenade under the locust trees on Front

The Fourth of July

Street were suddenly startled to see "Smoky Row" and the "Pinch-Gut" swarming with people: it was as if the whole district had boiled over, and the ragged straggling uproarious population of brothels and gambling houses alike came rushing up the Hill in battle order.

Once they reached the Bluff, however, their energies seemed to fail: the concentrated fury that had been born in the heavy atmosphere of their dens and alleys was as if dissipated in the rarer air of the upper level.

The mob swung jerkily through the streets, zigzagging, blundering. "Burn the Court House!" some one shouted. They set out running for the Public Square; they came to the solid brick structure sitting placidly among its trees and they halted, seesawing back and forth, irresolute. The Court House was unguarded; they might burn it if they chose but a sudden awe had struck them: the crowd ebbed away again.

So they went rambling all day through the town. Here and there bitter skirmishes developed: a merchant barred his doors—they were smashed into kindling and the mob flowed into the shop, looted it, and flowed out again; ladies surprised on some by-street screamed and scurried—less gentle ladies ran hooting after them, tearing frocks and pulling hair; armed citizens appeared in little quiet groups

279

at the doors of the statelier dwellings—armed gamblers and rowdies paraded in the dusty street outside the fences, jeering, threatening. . . .

A few shots were fired; a few shanties were burned; a great many curses were mouthed into empty air. And at last, toward nightfall, the crowd swung slowly down toward the River again, drinking, boasting.

Curiously, it was in their own "Gut" that they succeeded in doing the most damage: at the height of the orgy that followed the manifestation the Pedraza Hotel, the largest structure in the district and a hotbed of whores and gamblers, caught fire. And the townsmen, from their vantage-point on the Bluff, had the signal pleasure of watching the flames rise, spread roaring through the flimsy structure and finally destroy it utterly. Needless to say, on that occasion, the fire-engine company was conspicuously absent.

Meanwhile, in the settlements along the Trace, the actual purpose of the Clan itself had been revealed.

Toward the end of June, the wife of a wealthy planter named Latham, living near the town of Beattie's Bluff on the Big Black River in Madison County, Mississippi, stepped out on the north gallery of her home and overheard a curious conversation between a pair of negro slaves.

One of these was a nurse girl; the other was a big black field hand who had no business about the house, anyway: the girl was holding one of Mrs. Latham's babies in her arms. "But this here is such a pretty little baby!" she was saying earnestly. "You-all ought to know I never could kill that child!"

The black man shook his head doggedly. "When that day comes you-all got to, gal," he insisted. "Won't be no never-could about it. Us got to kill them all!"

But the girl still protested. "Go on kill all you-all wants," she retorted. "Won't nobody touch this lamb here. I won't let them touch him!"

Mrs. Latham, as soon as she had grasped the import of the conversation, had drawn back out of sight; now she slipped quietly away to tell her husband what she had heard. He ordered the girl to be brought immediately before him.

She came; her mind was already overweighted with the dark secret that had been confided to her: it needed only a stern look and a word from the master to make her tell all. An hour later, Latham was riding from one plantation to another among his neighbors, spreading the direful warning that plans were under way among the negroes for an uprising and a general massacre of the whites.

The Outlaw Years

A meeting was held. One by one, suspected negroes were dragged in and questioned. Fear and the whip soon had them babbling, but few could give more than the vaguest details of the scheme. It was not until several groping days had passed that the planters learned anything of the widespreading ramifications of the conspiracy.

It was a young black boy named Joe who first revealed the fact that white men had engineered the black uprising. "He said that the negroes were going to rise and kill all the whites on the Fourth, and that they had a number of white men at their head: some of them he knew by name, others he only knew when he saw them.

"He mentioned the following white men as actively engaged in the business: Ruel Blake, Doctors Cotton and Sanders, and many more, but could not call their names: and that he had seen others. He also gave the names of several slaves as ring leaders in the business, who were understood to be captains under these white men."

And he told how the negroes on each plantation were to kill their immediate masters with axes, hoes, clubs: how then they were to seize the arms in the houses and circle in toward the towns. Meeting there, they would ransack stores and dwelling; they would go on, killing whites and recruiting blacks, until they were strong enough to attack Natchez in force: so they would range up and down the River until they had the whole territory under their control.

He told how a site for general headquarters had been chosen, in the "Devil's Punch Bowl," a sunken swamp just north of Natchez. He stated that, though they planned to kill all the whites, they had been told that each negro might claim one white woman for himself: he added naïvely that "he had already picked out one for himself, and that he and his wife had quarreled over it, when he told her of his intention."

It was Murrel's plan of campaign all over again. The little group of planters at Beattie's Bluffs perceived immediately, with consternation, that they had uncovered something very deep and grave indeed.

On June 30, the nine or ten negroes who had been questioned were led out, roped hand to hand and leg to leg, to a grove of cottonwoods along the Big Black River and there hanged.

Next day, the gentlemen rode down to Livingston, chief town and county-seat of Madison County, to spread a more general warning.

At Livingston, a mass meeting was immediately held, and a "Committee of Safety" comprising thirteen members elected, with "power to bring before them any person or persons, either white or black,

283

and try in summary manner any person brought before them, with the power to hang or whip." Colonel H. D. Runnels was appointed chairman; patrols were instituted throughout the county. Sanders, Blake and Cotton, and other white men implicated by suspicion, were ordered arrested. The Committee began its delving into the packed black soil of ignorance and mistrust that had stirred so strangely beneath their feet.

Joshua Cotton was brought in: he was a smooth blank man, a New Englander who had come into the territory some twelve months before; he had settled at the Old Agency, down along the Trace; he had "hoisted a sign as a Steam Doctor," practicing that now abandoned form of therapeutics.

Nothing much was known against him. There was a rumor that he had tried to sell his wife to a man setting out for the Arkansaw country; the man, startled, had refused the proposition; soon after, Cotton's wife had suddenly disappeared. And now people were wondering if the woman had not been murdered.

But nothing could be proved. His partner, Sanders, had been seen at Beattie's Bluffs during the investigation there; he was supposed to have told some one there that Cotton was a great nigger-stealer, and that "he was mixed up in other tradings

The Fourth of July

with the niggers, too." But Sanders had suddenly vanished, and no one else appeared to confirm the rumor. The Committee stared at this man Cotton, so suddenly thrust forward to their attention, and tried to see his true figure against the background of suspicion and vague report.

They seemed to be getting nowhere. Cotton protested blandly, assuring them of his innocence: they were about to order his release when the missing Sanders was dragged in. He had been riding down to Vicksburg and had fallen in with a traveler: he had talked.

He had told of the conspiracy, and how his partner, a man named Cotton, was one of the ringleaders: "Cotton had wanted him to join them, but he would not." Instead, he was making off for Texas, to get out of harm's way. The traveler listened quietly; at the first town he had Sanders arrested, and sent back under guard.

Faced by the Committee, Sanders repeated his assertions: he said that Cotton was a nigger-stealer and a horse-thief; that he was one of the heads of an organization of cut-throats called "the Domestic Lodge," and that the members of this lodge were the men who had organized the whole negro rebellion. Cotton denied everything.

But now a newcomer appeared, a planter of the neighborhood, whipping in one of his own black boys before him: the slave had a confession to make. He told how, "one day, while hunting horses in a prairie, a white man had approached him, and the man began to ask him about his master: if he was a bad man? whether the negroes were whipped much? and how he would like to be free? He said the man took a drink of brandy with him, *and made him drink first.*"

They pointed out Cotton to him: "When he saw Cotton, he boldly exclaimed, 'That is the man who talked to me in the prairie!'"

Cotton "looked thunderstruck"; he offered no further denials; he seemed sunk in a daze of despondency. When they urged him, he willingly agreed to write out a full confession of his guilt.

"I was one of the principal men in bringing about the conspiracy," he wrote. "I am one of the Murrel clan, a member of what we call the Grand Council. I counseled with them twice; once near Columbus, this spring, and another time on an island in the Mississippi River.

"Our object in undertaking to excite the negroes to rebellion, was not for the purpose of liberating them, but for plunder. Blake's boy Peter had his duty assigned to him, which was, to get such negroes into the secret as he could trust, generally the most daring; but from the exposure of our plans in Stewart's pamphlet, we expected the citizens would be

The Fourth of July

on their guard at the time mentioned, that being the 25th of December next; and we determined to take them by surprise and try it on the night of the 4th of July, and it may yet be tried. . . ."

And he went on, to list the names of his fellow-conspirators: "All the names I now recollect who are deeply concerned, are Andrew Boyd, Albe Dean, William Sanders, two Rawsons of Hinds County . . . John and Wm. Earle, near Vicksburg in Warren county, Ruel Blake of Madison County. I have heard Blake say he would make his negroes help, and he was equal in command with me. Lunsford Barnes of this County; Thom. Anderson, below Clinton in Hinds county; John Rogers, near Benton, Yazoo County; Lee Smith of Hinds County, and John Ivy in Vernon. There are arms and ammunition deposited in Hinds County, near Raymond."

And he signed his name: "Joshua Cotton," and handed the document over to the Committee. And that afternoon he was led out under strong guard, and hanged. The judges had hastened his execution, in the hope that the news of quick and stern justice might frighten the others of the Clan, and Cotton himself seemed to concur in the opinion.

As he stood with the rope on his neck, some one asked him if he expected there would be trouble on the Fourth. He turned slowly and surveyed the speaker. "Yes," he said. "Unless the others learn that I have been hanged."

His last words were, "Take care of yourselves to-night and to-morrow night."

And the grim Committee went on with its work, digging deeper and deeper in the tangled roots of the conspiracy. It was sweaty work; they sat from nine in the morning until four at night and hour by hour through those sweltering days that preceded the Fourth men were led in, quaking and babbling or sullen and silent, were questioned, and were led out again, to be hanged.

Sanders was hanged. There had been no evidence against him except that Cotton included his name in the confession—and he stood there hysterically sobbing, pleading until the rope choked him—but they hanged him, anyway.

Albe Dean was hanged. He had been a lazy, shiftless roustabout; his trade, ostensibly, had been carpentering but he had seldom worked at it: no one knew much about him—who he was, where he came from, what he did with his time. When the posse set out for him they found him wandering in a swamp, vaguely seeking to escape. He died in dogged silence, neither admitting or denying his guilt, but he made one last request—that his name be kept secret: he said his father was a prominent man, and would be shamed to learn of his son's ending.

Lee Smith was hanged. They found him sitting in his own dooryard, cleaning a gun. He saw them coming for him, and made a leap for his pistols, inside the house. A shot halted him, and he stood there. "What is it?" he cried wildly. "Has Jo Cotton named me?" As they led him away, he made his escape, but that night he was caught again, furtively returning. He was hanged.

John Ivy and Andrew Boyd escaped to the swamps, with a pack of bloodhounds on their trail. Boyd was tracked down and captured and hanged; Ivy went plunging here and there through the canebrake—they could hear him ahead but they could never come up with him—and toward nightfall he stole a horse from a clearing beyond the swamp and got away.

He was one of the few who escaped. A posse came in with the two Earle brothers. William, the elder, needed little urging to make a full confession: he seemed to take a desperate pride in the fact that he had been an important member in the Clan. He explained their whole plan of campaign; he admitted that he was to have been Captain of all the forces in the Yazoo country. They told him he was going to be hanged; he looked thoughtful, and said, "Well, I would have done the same."

The Outlaw Years

It was too late to hang him that day; they put him in a room, to lie until next morning: when they came for him again they found him hanging from the top rung of a ladder propped against the wall, with a bandanna handkerchief for a rope. He was dead, and at news of his death his brother rejoiced. "I would never be in this scrape if it hadn't been for him," he said. "It was my brother that made a rascal out of me." He was hanged soon after, still blaming his brother for his own ending.

So they went, each man meeting death after the dictates of his own nature. William Earle had mentioned a man named Angus Donovan: Donovan was brought in. He had arrived in the country only a few weeks earlier but already he had acquired a reputation as a curious character. He was always hanging about with the negroes; now one man, an overseer on a large plantation, came forward to report a strange conversation he had had with the fellow.

He had been working a gang of niggers in a field, when Donovan approached him. "By God, sir! I wouldn't like to have your job," said Donovan. Asked why, he muttered, "Well, there is too much whipping needed." The overseer, surprised, replied that he only whipped a slave when he deserved it; Donovan had frowned: "Well," he went on. "You won't be using the whip much longer, at any rate.

The Fourth of July

Sir! This whipping and slave-driving will soon be stopped. Those negroes will be free as you and I, you'll see it. There are thousands of men, with money and ammunition all ready, to help them get free when the time comes."

The overseer, irritated, had sent him packing on his way; he had started off down the road and then returned again: "I am going to have a talk with those negroes," he shouted, trying to force his way into the field where they were working. "I am going to tell them something of their rights!" The other, brandishing his whip, had driven him away.

The Committee, listening to all this, concluded that Donovan had been "undoubtedly the emissary of those deluded fanatics at the North, the Abolitionists." And Donovan was led out like the others. They gave him time to pray, but he soon became frenzied and almost blasphemous. The rope cut him short. He was hanged.

Some weeks later, a letter came to his address. Donovan was by now rotting in the ditch where they had buried him. The letter was opened by the Committee: it was from his wife in Maysville, Kentucky, and he had evidently been arranging for her to join him at Livingston when he had been arrested. She wrote full of joy at the reunion: "O my dear Angus, it is a great consolation to me to think of seeing you again, and once more enjoying your company. . . . I hope you have laid up something to commence housekeeping with. . . . But I defer for the present . . and I subscribe myself, yours, affectionately, Mary."

Among those suspected, the name of Ruel Blake had been mentioned several times, and still men could hardly bring themselves to believe him guilty. For Blake himself was a land-owner, a slave-holder, a man of substance in the community: it seemed incredible that he should have joined a gang of ruffians in a plot to destroy the very class to which he belonged. In the end, it was through one of his own slaves that his guilt was brought out.

A curious detail of punctilio in the conduct of the investigation had obtained: though the Committee had the right to call out any man's slaves for question, the actual handling of the whip in the beating which was administered to "loosèn up" the negro's mind was always left, courteously, to the owner himself.

So now, when Blake's black boy, Peter, was hauled before the Committee, he was seized, stripped, bound like the others over the heavy table which served as whipping block; and then the whip was handed to Blake: "Make him talk," they said.

Blake took the whip, swung it up, brought it down on the boy's bare back; he was making a great deal

The Fourth of July

of play with his elbows; he seemed to be laying it on furiously but those men about him were experts in the art: it was obvious to all of them that there was no sting in his blows. He was only pretending to thrash the fellow.

Still no one suspected him, but they did come to the very definite conclusion that he was far too soft-hearted for his job. So Blake, somewhat protesting, was gently thrust aside. Another man, a Mr. Johnson, took the whip.

And now the heavy black-snake sang through the air, and the lash began its stinging dance on Peter's black back. At the first strong stroke the boy kept mum. At the second stroke his eyes began to roll about the room, staring for his master, and Blake himself, thrust back into the watching crowd, began to pace wildly to and fro—"He was under great agitation"—his eyes rolling as wildly as those of the tortured negro himself.

At the third stroke, Peter's mouth twitched and he began a sort of slobbering mumble; at the fourth stroke he let out a yell. And then they knew that his courage had broken. "Go on, Johnson!" some one cried. "He'll be talking now." Johnson drew back for the final burst of blows.

But at that instant Blake came shoving back through the crowd. He seized Johnson's arm, spun the man around: "You can't whip that boy of mine!"

he shouted in a frenzy. "Whoever wants to whip that boy has got to whip me first!"

For three days now the little committee room had been a theater of blood and passion. The yells of one negro had followed those of another, constantly echoing, until the very air seemed continually trembling with their tortured outcry. Black backs had crowded there, to be welted and torn by the cutting lash. White faces had stared; strange questions had been asked and stranger answers given, and the end of all had been the rope. The whole long grim proceeding had been a kind of masque of pain and brutal suffering and death and now the passions of the men who watched and worked there had been strained to the pitch where no human note remains.

So with Johnson. He looked once at the white face of Blake, staring frenzied; then, with hardly a pause, he brought the whip down again, full in the other's face.

Blake staggered back, then came rushing. Johnson met him: there was a flurry of blows, and then the two went rolling on the floor while the crowd hung greedily over them. In a moment, however, some of the saner bystanders interfered. This was a disgraceful proceeding, they said; they hauled Blake to his feet and rushed him outside. "Run for it," some one cried. "They're holding Johnson inside. If he gets loose he'll kill you sure."

A typical frontier hanging, "The whole population turned out to see it."
—*From a color lithograph by F. D. Salmson, about 1850.*

The Fourth of July

Blake ran, his face still streaming with blood. A crowd of the village youngsters took up the chase, hooting and pelting him with stones. Some way down the road a neighbor, Captain Thomas Hudnold, saw the rout and was moved to pity: he scattered the children, gave his own horse to Blake, blindly staggering: "Get away somewhere and lie low for a time," he advised him. "Then you better come back and apologize."

It was not until later that day, when they resumed questioning the negro boy Peter, that they learned that Blake would probably never come back. Blake was guilty, and the posses set out immediately in search of him, spurred on by an offer of five hundred dollars reward, dead or alive.

They found him in Natchez, hiding in one of the boatmen's taverns. They brought him back to his doom. And by now all the hatred of the town had centered on him; he was the last of the conspirators to be executed, and the whole population turned out to see him hanged. He died, protesting his innocence to the last.

So the clumsy mechanism of Murrel's mad plan was blocked at the very hub of all its movement; at its periphery, where it circled through the River towns, it had spent its force in no less futile fashion. It had all been like a travesty of Murrel's grandiose intentions—the straggled parading of those evil crusaders, their threats, their empty curses, their ultimate ineffectual withdrawals—and yet it had had its effect.

The underworld had shown its teeth, and though no bite had been felt the minds of those who had looked into its ugly jaws were still in consternation. People went about bewildered for a time, and then at last their anger rose.

In Vicksburg a great mass meeting was held, and the situation canvassed. "For years past, the gamblers have made our city their place of rendezvous. They support a large number of tippling-houses . . . no citizen is ever secure from their villainy. Our streets are ever resounding with the echoes of their drunken mirth. . . ." The time had come to end it all. A set of resolutions was offered, banishing them forever, and passed by unanimous acclaim.

Resolved: That a notice be given to all professional gamblers, that the citizens of Vicksburg are resolved to exclude them from this place and this vicinity; and that 24 hours notice be given them to leave the place.

Resolved: That all persons permitting faro-dealing in their houses, be also notified that they will be prosecuted therefor.

Resolved: That 100 copies of the foregoing resolutions be printed and stuck up at the corners of the streets—and that this publication be deemed notice.

They waited, grimly, for twenty-four hours, and then the townsmen descended on the shanties of the Landing. They found the gamblers barricaded in the tavern of John North, ready for battle.

In the crisis, a Dr. Hugh S. Bodley went forward seeking a parley. A shot from an upper window killed him, and the fight was on.

The townsmen won. In the final rush, five of the gamblers were captured, among them North himself, and the five were strung up instanter: they were hanged in the doorways along the street, and their bodies, by order, were left hanging for twenty-four hours, "as a warning against those that had escaped"; they were then cut down and buried in a ditch.

This was the first concerted action against the lawless, and it had a tremendous effect throughout the territory. "The news spread like wildfire through the Mississippi Valley, and was eagerly discussed by every fireside, at every crossroads store, and on every stage-coach throughout the South."

Until then it had been the law-abiding who spoke warily—"so strong had the Clan been, that no one was willing to run the risk of offending them"—but now a great flame of righteousness blazed everywhere. "It gave heart to the lovers of law and order. Committees were formed in every community from Cincinnati to New Orleans that had suffered from the thief and the cutthroat, and general notices issued for them to leave in 24 hours." The clean-up began.

Laws were strengthened and the police reenforced; where these were lacking, the citizenry itself banded together: "Every town along the River had its vigilant committee and patrol. . . . Strangers that entered the town were 'spotted,' until their business had been satisfactorily known to the guards."

Groups of men bound themselves together, in summary authority: "Know all men by these presents," they would proclaim, "that we have this day, jointly and severally, bound ourselves together as a Company of Rangers and Regulators . . . to rid the country of such as are dangerous to the welfare of this settlement, and generally to vindicate the law. . . ." They would sign the sheet, and then go forth to join the posses already harrying the outlaws.

Little quarter was shown: men who had lived by brutal murder deserved brutally to die, and sometimes the punishment meted out to them achieved an almost medieval ingenuity of torture. Thus once in Mississippi, an interesting variant of the usual whipping was evolved: instead of the snake-whip, nettles were used: "The man was taken to a place where nettles were known to grow in great luxuriance, completely stripped, and so lashed with them that he took it as a hint not to be neglected, left the country and was never heard of again."

Or, later, near the town of Randolph, Tennessee: it had been learned that Murrel's great headquarters had been in the Arkansaw swamps just across the way, and now Randolph was especially vigilant. It even maintained a night patrol, and one night, creeping through the bottoms, the guardsmen surprised a boatload of suspects—"an old gray-haired lark and two younger, father and sons"—rowing silently into the bayou.

They were tied, tried on the spot "under the code of Judge Lynch"; the gray hairs of the old man won them all a lesser verdict than hanging. "They were sentenced to be denuded of every vestige of clothing, stretched across a cotton bale and striped with a $3\frac{1}{2}$ inch cowhide at intervals, until day began to break, the old man to receive two licks to the boys one."

So they were beaten, alternately, until the anguished dawn: even then, the punishment was not done. They had been further sentenced: "that when day began to dawn, they be taken to their boat, stark naked, tied hand and foot and fast to the bottom of the boat, face upwards, gagged, with a placard posted upon each of their foreheads—the boat to be carried out in the middle of the current and set adrift without oars. . . ." The account, with its grim particularization of the punishment, shows the bitterness at work in men's minds, and every detail of the sentence was carried out.

"The sentence was fully executed, and their upturned faces greeted the first rays of the morning sun." They were set drifting, already aching after the whip, to burn with thirst or starve with hunger, to be snagged, overturned, drowned—nobody even bothered to inquire what had become of them.

These were savage reprisals, but perhaps such measures were needed, for the savage men they had to deal with. And the great sweep went on, driving the outlaws westward across the River, into the unsettled regions beyond. The ultimate effect of the movement of course is doubtful: many of the exiled bandits came filtering back again and certainly in the great days of steamboating soon to follow the gamblers found the River as rich a field as ever it had been before.

But the immediate results were tremendous. Now definitely law had broken the back of lawlessness: here and there the highwayman might operate or the murderer strike his victim down, but such incidents would be scattered and their importance, henceforth, local. The day of the great Land Pirates was done.

The Fourth of July

Murrel had been the last and the greatest, and the crowning paradox of his fantastic career lies in the fact that it had been his own scheming that brought about the ruin of them all.

He lay in the Penitentiary. He served his term, working as did the other eighty convicts there, at the prison occupations of "shoemaking, lathing, tailoring, coopering, carding." For a time he studied law, and then he turned to Scripture: he had the ambition to be a minister when he got out.

But long before his sentence ended, the man's mind had cracked. When at last the prison doors opened and he emerged again, it was as an invalid and practically an imbecile. His wife had gone, his lands had been claimed; his brother had vanished. He, too, in his turn, disappeared: his final outcome —his death, his place of burial—unknown.

But perhaps, in the final vanquishing of the robber gangs, a stronger force than even the fury of the aroused populace had been at work. The bandits had been born of the wilderness: its thickets and swamps had been the background and its lonely trails the scene of all their operations. And now the wilderness itself was vanishing; the scene had shifted, and like actors on a vacant stage they were left with no background for the consummation of their plotting.

The Outlaw Years

Steam conquered the River. Even before Murrel had come out of his prison, steam had conquered the wilderness. Travel straightened its path and increased its speed; rails linked the cities in a network no outlaw could hope to break. Times changed, and with their changing even the old memories were forgotten.

The Cave-in-Rock remained to be pointed out—a dark cleft thick-grown with bushes in the yellow cliff—as the steamboat surged along the shore; Wolf Island still lay with its heavy hood of willows in the middle of the stream; the pathway of the Wilderness Road and the Natchez Trace might still be discerned winding here and there through the forests back of the plantations: but the men who haunted them—Hare, and the bloody Harpes, Mason and the proud fantastic Murrel—had been forgotten, and even the background of wilderness and lonely striving that had bred them—the dark passions, the bitter abnegations, the solitary lives and the wild convocations of those early days—had been fading in men's minds.

END

BIBLIOGRAPHY

An Explanation

This seems to be the proper place to explain a practise followed in this book which may seem open to objection. Throughout, I have identified neither the sources for statements of fact nor even the authorship of quotations from those sources, when incorporated in the text. Still further, I have sometimes made elisions in the quoted texts without bothering to indicate the hiatus by the customary row of dots, and occasionally I have gone so far as to make slight changes (as the tense of a verb, or the substitution of a name for a pronoun, etc.) when such changes seemed to make for clarity or convenience. When the authorities conflicted, I have chosen the version among them which seemed most probable and most in keeping with the spirit of the time. Thus, there are at least a dozen versions of Big Harpe's death, and almost as many varying descriptions of the man himself (i.e., red hair, black hair, skin dark, sallow, sunburned and pale); I chose that which seemed to me to fit the man best.

In all this, I was moved by no other purpose than the one of general convenience. This book was designed for the general reader, and it seemed to me therefore that the elaborate accuracy of the student would here be out of place.

Certainly, I intended no disrespect to the sources

themselves. The books of reminiscence and of gossip written by the early settlers are now almost totally neglected by the casual reader, yet they form a curious chapter in the history of American letters. They are rich in anecdote: even in their faults—of stilted phraseology and romantic statement—they reveal the temper of their day; the best of them have a garrulous and peculiarly engrossing quality of their own, fully as quaint and naïvely amusing as the European memoirs of the Eighteenth and Nineteenth Centuries which we are all so fond of having on our library shelves.

More people ought to read them. In the list below I have mentioned only those consulted in the preparation of this book; although there are dozens of others equally interesting not referred to by me, or not bearing on the subject of the Land Pirates, I have taken the liberty of commenting here and there on some of the titles, to be of such help as might be to anyone interested in reading further among them.

Albach, James R., *The Annals of the West.*
    W. S. Haven; Pittsburgh. 1857.
Ashe, Thomas, *Travels In America.*
    London. 1808. (Very interesting chronicle of an astonished Englishman, on a trip down the Mississippi.)
Audubon, John James, *Delineation of American Scenery and Character.*
    G. A. Bakerer Co.; New York City. 1926. (A series of sharp sketches of frontier life, from the naturalist's own experience.)
Baird, Rev. Doctor Robert, *A View of the Valley of the Mississippi.*
    H. S. Tanner; Philadelphia. 1834. (From a clergyman's point of view.)

Bibliography

Baldwin, Joseph G., *The Flush Times of Alabama and Mississippi.*
Sumer Whitney & Co.; San Francisco. 1883. (A lawyer during
the cotton boom.)

Breazeale, H. S., *Life As It Is.*
James Williams; Knoxville, Tenn. 1842. (Full of random
reminiscences.)

Brooke, Henry K., *The Highwaymen and Pirates' Own Book.*
J. B. Perry: New York City. 1845. (Like the title.)

Chambers, Henry E., *Mississippi Valley Beginnings.*
G. P. Putnam's Sons; New York City. 1922.

Coale, Edward J., *Trials of the Mail Robbers.*
E. J. Coale; Baltimore. 1818.

Cobb, Joseph B., *Mississippi Scenes.*
A. Hart; Philadelphia. 1851.

Collins, Lewis, *History of Kentucky.*
Collins & Co.; Covington, Ky. 1874. (Source book of early
chronicles.)

Cramer, Zadock, *The Navigator.*
Cramer, Spear & Eichbaum; Pittsburgh. 1811. ("Containing
directions for navigating the Monongahela, Allegheny, Ohio
& Mississippi Rivers, with an ample account of these much
admired waters.")

Davis, James D., *History of the City of Memphis.*
Hite, Crumpton & Kelly; Memphis, Tenn. 1873. (One of
the best.)

Davis, Reuben, *Recollections of Mississippi and the Mississippians.*
Houghton Mifflin & Co.; Boston. 1889.

Devol, George H., *Forty Years a Gambler on the Mississippi.*
Devol & Haines; Cincinnati, O. 1887.

Dunbar, Seymour, *A History of Travel in America.*
Bobbs-Merrill Co.; Indianapolis. 1915. (Standard for the
subject and very interesting.)

Duvallon, Berquin, *Vue de la Colonie Espagnole du Mississippi.*
Duvallon; Paris. 1803. (A Parisian in the provinces. There is
a translation published in New York by L. R. Riley & Co.,
1806, but it takes the heart out of the original.)

The Outlaw Years

Fulkerson, H. S., *Early Days in Mississippi.*
  Vicksburg Printing & Publishing Co.; Vicksburg, Miss. 1885.
  (Excellent book of gossip.)
Glazier, Capt. Willard, *Down The Great River.*
  Hubbard Bros.; Philadelphia. 1883.
Gould, E. W., *Fifty Years on the Mississippi.*
  Nixon-Jones; St. Louis. 1889. (Full of anecdote.)
Guild, Josephus Conn, *Old Times in Tennessee.*
  Tavel, Eastman & Howell; Nashville. 1878. (The best of all.)
Hall, James, *Sketches of the History, Life and Manners in the
  West.*
  Hubbard & Edmands; Cincinnati. 1834.
Hall, James, *The West.*
  H. W. Derby & Co.; Cincinnati. 1848.
Harper, Lillie DuPuy VanCulin, *Colonial Men and Times.*
  Innes & Sons; Philadelphia. 1916. (Contains the Journal of
  Col. Daniel Trabue and a list of his rich relations.)
Howard, H. R., *The History of Virgil A. Stewart.*
  Harper & Bros.; New York City, 1836.
Ingraham, Joseph Holt, *The Southwest by a Yankee.*
  Harper & Bros.; New York City. 1835. (Interesting travels
  of a rather biased observer.)
Lloyd, James T., *Lloyd's Steamboat Directory.*
  J. T. Lloyd & Co.; Cincinnati. 1856. (Almanach of early
  doings on the River.)
McConnell, J. L., *Western Characters.*
  Redfield; New York City. 1853.
Morris, Eastin, *The Tennessee Gazetteer.*
  W. Hassell Hunt & Co.; Nashville, Tenn. 1834.
Palmer, John, *Journal of Travels.*
  Sherwood, Neely & Sons; London. 1818.
Phelan, James, *History of Tennessee.*
  Houghton Mifflin & Co.; Boston. 1888.
"Police Gazette, Editor of," *The Pictorial Life and Adventures
  of John A. Murrel.*
  T. B. Peterson & Bros.; Philadelphia. 1848.
Power, Tyrone, *Impressions of America.*
  Richard Bentley; London. 1836. (An actor's amusing tales.)

Bibliography

Ramsey, James G. M., *Annals of Tennessee.*
    Lippincott, Grambo & Co.; Philadelphia. 1853. (Source book.)
Rothert, Otto A., *The Outlaws of Cave-in-Rock.*
    Arthur H. Clark Co.; Cleveland, O. 1924. (Very interesting.
    Authority for the Harpes and Mason; particularly valuable
    for his researches among contemporary newspapers, etc., for
    reports of their crimes, and among the court records of the
    proceedings at their trials. I have followed his account, and
    quoted from him, with respect to these episodes.)
Rowland, Dunbar, *History of Mississippi.*
    S. J. Clarke Co.; Chicago. 1925.
Rowland, Dunbar, *Official Letter Books of W. C. C. Claiborne.*
    State Dept. of Archives & History; Jackson, Miss. 1917.
Rowland, Eron Opha, *History of Hinds County.*
    For the Mississippi Historical Society; Jackson, Miss.
    1922.
Speed, Thomas, *The Wilderness Road.*
    John P. Morton & Co., for the Filson Club; Louisville, Ken-
    tucky. 1886.
Thwaites, Reuben Gold, *The Colonies.*
    Longmans, Green & Co.; London. 1913.
Thwaites, Reuben Gold, *The Ohio Valley Press before the War
    of 1812-15.*
    Davis Press; Worcester, Mass. 1909.
Trollope, Mrs. Francis Milton, *The Domestic Manners of the
    Americans.*
    Whittaker, Treacher & Co.; London. 1832. (The experiences
    of a very refined lady among the barbarians.)
Walton, Augustus Q., *A History of the Detection, Conviction,
    Life and Designs of John A. Murrel, the Great Western
    Land Pirate.*
    George White; Athens, Tenn. 1835.
Watts, William Courtney, *The Chronicles of a Kentucky Settle-
    ment.*
    G. P. Putnam's Sons; New York City. 1897.
Williams, J. S., *Old Times in West Tennessee.*
    W. G. Cheeney; Memphis, Tenn. 1873. (Amusing reminis-
    cences.)
    Also, various publications of the Ohio Archaeological and His-

The Outlaw Years

torical Society, the Mississippi Historical Society; various contemporary newspapers, as the New Orleans *Picayune,* the New York *Columbian,* the Cincinnati *Daily Gazette,* etc.; various maps, pamphlets, stage-route guides, etc., etc.